# WHEN TEARS SING

D1451910

# WHEN TEARS SING

## The Art of Lament
## in Christian Community

**William Blaine-Wallace**

ORBIS BOOKS
Maryknoll, New York 10545

Founded in 1970, Orbis Books endeavors to publish works that enlighten the mind, nourish the spirit, and challenge the conscience. The publishing arm of the Maryknoll Fathers and Brothers, Orbis seeks to explore the global dimensions of the Christian faith and mission, to invite dialogue with diverse cultures and religious traditions, and to serve the cause of reconciliation and peace. The books published reflect the views of their authors and do not represent the official position of the Maryknoll Society. To learn more about Orbis Books, please visit our website at www.orbisbooks.com.

Copyright © 2020 by William Blaine-Wallace

Published by Orbis Books, Box 302, Maryknoll, NY 10545-0302.

All rights reserved.

No part of this publication may be reproduced or transmitted in any form or by any means, electronic or mechanical, including photocopying, recording, or any information storage and retrieval system, without prior permission in writing from the publisher.

Queries regarding rights and permissions should be addressed to: Orbis Books, P.O. Box 302, Maryknoll, NY 10545-0302.

The permissions listed in the back matter of this book represent an extension of this copyright page.

Manufactured in the United States of America
Manuscript editing and typesetting by Joan Weber Laflamme.

**Library of Congress Cataloging-in-Publication Data**

Names: Blaine-Wallace, William, 1951– author.
Title: When tears sing : the art of lament in Christian community / William Blaine-Wallace.
Description: Maryknoll, NY : Orbis Books, 2020. | Includes bibliographical references and index. | Summary: "Through narrative examples, the author describes "lament" as the act of bringing more of our lived experience into congregational and communal life"— Provided by publisher.
Identifiers: LCCN 2019031326 (print) | LCCN 2019031327 (ebook) | ISBN 9781626983670 (paperback) | ISBN 9781608338313 (ebook)
Subjects: LCSH: Public worship. | Grief—Religious aspects—Christianity. | Laments.
Classification: LCC BV15 .B575 2020 (print) | LCC BV15 (ebook) | DDC 264—dc23
LC record available at https://lccn.loc.gov/2019031326
LC ebook record available at https://lccn.loc.gov/2019031327

*For the Missing Generation,*
*the 235,000 people who died of AIDS prior to 1993,*
*and those who loved and cared for them.*

# Contents

# 6
# Choir Rehearsal
## *Practicing Lament*

# 7
# The Shadow of Paradise

**8**

## Stubborn Melancholy
### *Lessons from Emmanuel Church*

**Epilogue**
## The Community of Saints

# Acknowledgments

Writing about lament is something like bricolage—art created by materials lying about and near at hand. My material is the lived experiences of shared sorrow, suffering, and trauma accumulated over the course of several decades. Bricolage, as testimonial performance, requires witnesses who engage. I am deeply grateful to Victoria Blaine-Wallace, Regina Knox, Mike Shea, Sharon Thornton, and Jerry Wallace, who, during the writing of *When Tears Sing*, stayed the course of a long and hardy testifier-witness relation. They were invaluable and steadfast conversational partners.

I am thankful for those whose ideas and reflections provided new and renewed insights and energy for the writing—Deryck Durston, Sara Gavit, Joy Howard, Mary Ann Hoy, Brett Johnson, Tim McFadden, Larry Moore, Jennifer Reece, Carl Straub, and Pam Werntz. I am very grateful to Jill Brennan O'Brien, my editor at Orbis Books. Jill had the heart to let me write the book I wanted and needed to write before she took her wise and deft hand to the text.

I offer a big *AMEN!* for my years at Grady Hospital in Atlanta. Time spent in the Grady hospice program and at the Grady AIDS clinic was a time out of time, holy time, church. At Grady, my belief in the relational heart of lament changed to trust. Trust incites passion fiery enough to write about. Grady remains an icon of the heart of God to which I regularly pray for courage, insight, direction, hope.

Victoria, my spouse, besides being a formative witness, is a relationally vulnerable and resilient partner, which makes for, among other things, a great conversational partnership in regard to lament and much more. I learn from her what it means to go on together amid life-the-way-it-really-is. And, *bravo* to our children and grandchildren, who, during my months of writing, regularly coaxed me out of my study, emptied my head of all things *Tears*, and refreshed my spirit. My desire for them and all future generations of God's children is that they come to experience shared sorrow, suffering, and trauma as the nearest and strongest source of their renewal and the best hope to reconcile and heal a broken world.

## Introduction

# God's Peculiar Wealth

*May those who sow in tears reap with shouts of joy!*

—PSALM 126:5

## A Society of the Fragile and Resilient

Several years ago, the parish I served in Boston repointed the mortar between the stones of the church's tired facade. The chairperson of the building committee asked my spouse, Victoria, a graphic designer, to create a construction sign to announce the renovation. The parish's physical plant is on Newbury Street, the toniest street in town. Victoria created a sign that was more "boutique" than routine, something to catch the eye of the thousands of people who walked by the property each day. Her sign centered on words by Tennessee Williams, which he chose for his gravestone: *The violets in the mountains have broken the rocks.*[1]

The quotation became something of a mantra for the parish and a gift to those who passed by, an arresting gift for a few. One passerby, a friend from the neighborhood who remained on the fringes of the parish out of distaste for religion, sent this note about the sign:

---

[1] Tennessee Williams, *Camino Real* (New York: New Directions Books, 1953).

*xiii*

Last summer, I saw for the first time the quote on the church lawn. At first my mind was confused by the words and I didn't consciously understand the sentence. And, then, seconds later, I was overcome by such intense sadness at the realization of what the words meant—almost incomprehensible to my conscious mind, yet at a cellular level my being understood—and my tears fell uncontrollably. I began to play a game with myself of reading the words over and over to see when I would finally be able to read them without crying—it never happened. To me the words meant that this delicate, innocent beauty—the violets—were such pure goodness, that even though they were fragile, tiny, almost meaningless to some, these beautiful, innocent little violets kept growing and multiplying and their light and beauty broke open the hard, cold, impenetrable darkness of the rock. The realization that light, goodness, beauty, is so powerful that it is capable of breaking the hard, cold darkness is overwhelmingly emotionally jarring. Bill, is this something akin to God?[2]

Yes. And God declares, with open arms, our citizenship in the society of fragile and resilient people. We may not think we are eligible to vote. Yet God knows the troubles we've seen, and the troubles we cannot or will not let ourselves see—"That very Spirit intercedes with sighs too deep for words" (Rom 8:26). God also knows the enduring and resolute strength we discover when we bring our vulnerability into relation.

In the society of fragile and resilient people, shared sorrow, suffering, and trauma are transposed into ironic, immeasurable joy. Ironic because we do not readily imagine joy to emerge from

---

[2] William Blaine-Wallace, "A Pastoral Psychology of Lament: Pastoral Method, Priestly Act, Prophetic Witness" (PhD diss., Catholic University of Brabant [Tilburg, the Netherlands], 2009), 12–13.

shared pain. Immeasurable because the depths of joy cannot be plumbed. Joy, in the language of T. S. Eliot, is "a hint half guessed."[3]

Tears express this community's ecclesiology. Tears are the heart of its civility. A chorus of tears expresses church at its finest. Tears are the church's surest balm and verve in what novelist Walker Percy, almost five decades ago, in the first sentence of his unnervingly prophetic novel *Love in the Ruins*,[4] called "these dread latter days of the old violent beloved U.S.A., in the Christ-forgetting Christ-haunted death-dealing Western World." *When Tears Sing* is a commentary on and explication of the music of shared sorrow, suffering, and trauma.

## The Strong Tug of Sufficiency

Though we belong to the society of the fragile and resilient, we are often slow to embrace God's invitation for us to bring the more broken dimensions of ourselves into relation. It's as if we are asked to accept an invitation to abandon ourselves, to take leave of the inordinate amount of compensatory activity invested in sustaining a thin wherewithal—the polished veneer of an intact self. We have received the grace of collective vulnerability. We know sufficiency's short half-life—the attainment of an adequate life can be fleeting and is an ever-moving target. Still, the content and pace of our lives presume a greater trust in buffers and borders that secure our material and relational property. In America, the Benedictine balance of work and prayer as the heart of community is privatized. While hard to confess, the *labora* of my daily life reflects a popular mid-nineteenth-century *ora*: "Lord bless Me. My wife. Our son

---

[3] T. S. Eliot, "Four Quartets: The Dry Salvages," in *The Complete Poems and Plays 1909–1950* (New York: Harcourt Brace, 1980), 136.

[4] Walker Percy, *Love in the Ruins* (New York: Farrar, Straus and Giroux, 1971), 3.

John. His wife. Us Four, no more. Amen."[5] We are cultivated to attain, hold onto, and take back sufficiency when it abandons us.

We strive to have and to hold onto enough to sustain an adequate level of existence. Why not? The issue is what we determine to be adequate. What constitutes adequacy is often determined by the tribe to which we belong. The couple who lives "off the grid" just over the hill from our farm in the western foothills of Maine has one idea of what constitutes enough. The family who jets to its summer home in Bar Harbor has another idea. We want to belong. Belonging demands attention to persona, how we seek to mirror what the tribe privileges.

During the late 1980s, I spent weekdays stewarding a hospice program at Grady Hospital in Atlanta. The King Center and Ebenezer Baptist Church were just around the corner. On the ninth floor a team of caregivers and volunteers oversaw the dying of mostly impoverished African Americans with end-stage cancer and younger white men with AIDS. The commonality of death sculpted two communities unfamiliar with each other into what was, for me, my closest experience of "the beloved community."[6] I spent my weeknights and weekends at home on what citizens of Atlanta proper call the Powdered Donut, the city's outer circle of white enclaves. During the commute home, as I passed Stone Mountain, a sanctuary of the Ku Klux Klan, five miles from my subdivision, I put on the mask of the white middle class.

## A Spirituality of Scarcity

We renounce our place in the commonwealth of the fragile and resilient in order to bank enough sufficiency to buffer ourselves from unanticipated factors and events that impinge upon us. The

---

[5] "My Wife and My Wife's Son," *Harper's Weekly,* February 8, 1868, 91.

[6] Popularized by Martin Luther King Jr., the "beloved community" is the idea of a society based on justice, equality, and love of one's neighbor.

problem, a spiritual one, is our belief that there is a fixed amount of resources to go around. Jesus reminds us, in the parable of the rich fool (Lk 12:13–21), that we fill our barns in the service of a holy scarcity. "And I will say to my soul, 'Soul, you have ample goods laid up for many years'" (v. 19a). Sacred regard for scarcity suggests that the cosmos is complete. Creation is a zero-sum game. Get what we can while we can.

## A Spirituality of the Self

Our devotion to scarcity propels us to secure and protect a self-sufficient identity resonant with North America's escalating trust in rugged individualism and independence. Over the last fifty years many trees have been sacrificed for the production of self-help books. Huge amounts of time and money have been lost to the quest to find oneself. A great deal of therapy has been aimed at acquiring a more bounded, "individuated," actualized self. And, as if that is not enough to wear us out, we try on different selves.

Sociologist Zygmunt Bauman writes about "momentary identities." One's identity is "for today until-further-notice."[7] There are multitudes of promises, ideologies, products, regimens, allegiances, and spiritualities vying to suspend our search and claim our souls for a while. The quest to discover one's self and to try on different selves suggests that the self's primary relation is with itself, at the expense of relation with others.

This is not necessarily bad. Modernity's birth of the *subjective I* created the possibility of self-examination as the spring from which one may determine the shape of a faithful life. Medieval peasants were not that concerned with who they were, might be, or could become as a child of God. They mostly knew what they should do, where they could get help doing it, and who they could go

---

[7] Zygmunt Bauman, *Morality, Immorality, and Other Life Strategies* (Stanford, CA: Stanford University Press, 1992), 167.

to for forgiveness and penance when they did not do it. On the other hand, the early years of modernism offered Martin Luther more "space" for a fierce and prolonged existential wrestling with the nature of salvation, and with the question: What does it mean to be a child of God?

Modernity also offered greater possibilities for examining what it means to be a self-in-relation.[8] Luther's laborious engagement with what constitutes being a child of God led him to give almost sacramental status to the grace that is "the mutual conversation and consolation of brethren."[9] My good friend echoes Luther: "Whether to take the plunge into relation with another person doesn't turn on any reasoned process at all, but on the self we've somehow become. That's why some of us run into burning buildings and others run from sick friends."

## A Morality of the Other

Bauman offered more than a diagnosis of the postmodern self; he proposed a view of the self that is expressive of those who run into burning buildings. Bauman situates this self in the moral philosophy of Emmanuel Levinas. For Levinas, the self is "I being *for* the Other, I bearing *responsibility* for the Other."[10] This is more ontological, who we are, than teleological, what we are supposed to do. Relation to the Other is what it means to be human, and the self remains human by living for others.[11] Levinas, over the years, has figured large in my own contemplations on the self-in-relation. I further develop Levinas's moral philosophy later in the book.

---

[8] Arthur W. Frank, *The Wounded Storyteller: Body, Illness, and Ethics*, 2nd ed. (Chicago: University of Chicago Press, 2013), 14.

[9] Paul Timothy McCain, ed., *Concordia: The Lutheran Confessions* (St. Louis: Concordia Publishing, 2007), 319.

[10] Bauman, *Morality, Immorality, and Other Life Strategies*, 42.

[11] Frank, *The Wounded Storyteller*, 15.

The society of fragile and resilient people is composed of selves, who try and favor living for one another. A foundational premise of this book is that "I being *for* the other, I bearing *responsibility* for the other" is the more moral path. The path is countercultural, an alternative and prophetic position. We need one another to help us stay on the path.

Moreover, I find that life offered for the Other is not a martyred life. When I prayerfully behold the tear-gassed child screaming at our nation's southwest border, I bestow upon her the authority to reorder my priorities. I am released from obligation and freed for engagement. The moral is transposed to the mystic.

## The Dread of Impermanence

Praying the relational self strengthens our trust in the beauty of what is constant.[12] James Baldwin writes that the constants of life are relational: "birth, struggle, death, and so is love, though we may not always think so."[13] The quest to find and trust the beauty of these relational constants requires time and daily reorientation to patience and attention. The parable of the rich barn builder (Lk 12:13–21) is a timeless story of the human compulsion to outrun death and, in so doing, to disregard what matters. Daily prayer keeps before us a struggle original to each of us and our relations—the tendency to take for granted, leave behind, triage, and hand off to professional caregivers the dynamics of birth, struggle, death, and love. Baldwin continues:

> Perhaps the whole root of our trouble, the human trouble, is that we will sacrifice all the beauty of our lives, will imprison ourselves in totems, taboos, crosses, blood sacrifices, steeples,

---

[12] James Baldwin, *The Fire Next Time* (New York: Vintage International, 1993; original, New York: The Dial Press, 1963), 91.

[13] Ibid., 92.

mosques, races, armies, flags, nations, in order to deny the fact of death, which is the only fact we have. It seems to me that one ought to rejoice in the fact of death—ought to decide, indeed, to *earn* one's death by confronting with passion the conundrum of life.[14]

## A Domesticated *Koinonia*

Our desire for citizenship in the society of the fragile and resilient ones, once it has passed through the sieve of sufficiency, often comes out as something like leftover grits. We tend to settle for and expect little more than lukewarm offerings to give or receive from neighbors. Our obeisance before the national idol of sufficiency dulls our desire for *koinonia*.

But here and there our desire for participation in the society of the fragile and resilient ones is quickened. Life-the-way-it-really-is[15] blemishes or topples the idol of sufficiency. We long for hearty community. But soon enough, life-the-way-it-might-be, what John Douglas Hall names as North America's "officially optimistic society,"[16] stimulates us to re-enthrone the idol of sufficiency.

This back-and-forth dynamic between the desire for sufficiency and the longing for *koinonia* is exhausting. Weary, we defer to self-sufficiency at the expense of community. We shelve the interdependent commerce of God that quiets the autonomy-laden priorities, claims, and goals we set for ourselves, desire for our loved ones, and expect from elected leaders. The more evidence we have to trust

---

[14] Ibid., 91–92.

[15] "Life-the-way-it-really-is" is a phrase I first heard in the "basic training" course of The Ecumenical Institute, an autonomous division of the Church Federation of Greater Chicago, which, in 1964, was incorporated as a nonprofit organization in the State of Illinois.

[16] John Douglas Hall, "How My Mind Has Changed," *The Christian Century* 127, no. 8 (September 7, 2010): 35.

the web of life usually does not move us to significantly reorder our priorities. No wonder, then, that Jesus's persistent appeal for his disciples to lose their lives was received more as a threat than a possibility. It is hard to hear Jesus's offer for us to lose our lives as a gift rather than as a demand.

Furthermore, our consumer society works to keep sufficiency just beyond our grasp so that we will keep grabbing for it. I am continuously urged to replace my latest and no longer greatest cell phone or coffee maker, both of which became obsolete soon after they were removed from the box. We are trained like the grey-hounds at the track to chase the forever-out-of-reach, mechanically propelled rabbit. No wonder that it takes loss and tragedy to wake us up, if only for a while.

James Baldwin's piercing indictment of white dominance in a radio dialogue with Reinhold Niebuhr in the aftermath of the September 1963 bombing of the 16th Street Baptist Church, which made martyrs of four little girls, remains far too relevant more than a half century later:

> The nature of life forces you in, in any extremity, any extreme, to discover what you really live by, whereas most Americans have been for so long, so safe and sleepy, that they don't any longer have any real sense of what they live by. I think they really think it may be Coca-Cola.[17]

## A Lukewarm Church

The North American church honors the idol of sufficiency. Church trusts sufficiency more than vulnerability, and it does so for reasons that make sense. We want to survive. Of late, our trust has been

---

[17] "The Protestant Hour" (Atlanta: The Protestant Radio and Television Center, Inc., 1963), quoted in James Cone, *The Cross and the Lynching Tree* (Maryknoll, NY: Orbis Books, 2011), 54.

rattled by the erosion of our relatively sufficient existence as post-Christian North America places us more at the margins of daily life. The first-world church is losing body mass. We experience the deterioration of attendance, membership, property, seminaries, power, and influence. We seek to turn around our losses. We want our lives back.

I believe that the church will not be restored to what it once was. I cannot imagine effective therapies, new "clinical trials" returning us to the more substantial days that were the last half of the twentieth century. My doubts are not fresh news. For a generation, emerging and progressive church movements have broken new ground for a renewed, or what we might call an ancient, pre-Constantine orthodoxy. There is a budding movement toward a more relation-based body of Christ.

## A Spirituality of Tears

A spirituality of tears advances the church's renewal. A spirituality of tears privileges vulnerability over sufficiency, relation over autonomy. A vulnerable and relational body of Christ exposes an emaciated assertion about existence: life is good until bad things happen. The duality of good and bad leaves gnawing questions about the nature of God. Is God too small or am I too bad? Moreover, the dichotomy of good and evil propagates ineffective responses to a world in crisis—"my truth is better than your truth" begets the "axis of evil," which begets "might is right." As perverse as this may seem, our tax monies fund it, and, in the end, little noise is made about it.

The relational heart of a spirituality of tears expresses an existence that transcends good, bad, and in between. Recently I was called to the home of a ninety-five-year-old woman who was actively dying. The house was full of family sitting vigil with their beloved matriarch. A young woman, the great-granddaughter, held her four-day-old baby boy. She walked to the side of the bed and placed the child on the chest of his great-great-grandmother. They seemed to be of one breath. Here was an icon of several generations of family relation. An accounting of family life would include many manifestations and variations of good, bad, and in between, with plenty of commentary on who has been good, bad, and in between. But at this moment, the ledger dissolved into a prayerful "Amen."

A spirituality of tears applies a holy "this-ness" to existence. Hurt, disillusionment, melancholia, loss, anguish, inadequacy, and trauma are not extraneous or peripheral visitations. They are integral parts of daily life. Moreover, the legions of sisters and brothers who have suffered trauma bear a disruption of personhood, an indelible spiritual crisis. Trauma is not an event that takes place at a particular time. Trauma "is an event that continues, that persists in the present. Trauma is what does not go away. It persists in symptoms that live on in the body and in the intrusive fragments of memories that return."[18] Deacon Julius Lee, staring at the foundation of what was his home before Hurricane Katrina, says, "The storm is gone, but the 'after the storm' is always here."[19]

When the life-giving and life-taking dimensions of lived experience are of a whole, not segregated like sheep and goats, we are less likely to see daily life as a riddle for God to explain or fix. We are apt to pray more simple and relational intentions that are answered through community. Relation is a prayer for forbearance answered.[20] Forbearance borne of relation is more and different than merely holding on and getting through. It arouses a more quietly offered and deeply experienced "Alleluia!"

---

[18] Shelly Rambo, *Trauma and Recovery: A Theology of Remaining* (Louisville, KY: Westminster John Knox Press, 2010), 2.

[19] Quoted in ibid., 1.

[20] I am grateful to my priest colleague and friend Sara Gavit for her insights regarding godly forbearance.

A spirituality of tears reorients and enriches what we mean by grief. Grief is more than what we experience and survive in times of bigger loss—death, broken relation, transition, loss of health, loss of work. Grief is a more reflective measuring of our lives both during and between times of bigger loss. Grief is prayerful attention, an awareness, acknowledgment, and embrace of life-the-way-it-really-is. Grief also pays attention to the many ways we avoid, deflect, and defend against life-the-way-it-really-is.

A turn toward a spirituality of tears is less about repentance, a turn from wrong to right, than a conversion begun and sustained by slowing down enough to see how our devotion to sufficiency distances us from God and neighbor. Close attention to one another amid life-the-way-it-really-is bridges the distance between self, God, and neighbor. Consolation and solidarity rise from and reside in the space between self, God, and neighbor. God rises among us. Resurrection is not a release from existence, not "an ecclesiastical projection of the ideology of success that drives the American dream."[21] Resurrection is near to and of existence, a chapter in the theology of the cross,[22] an emerging, convivial joy that begins in, transpires among, and vivifies the community of the bent and broken.

Barbara Holmes makes art of joy:

> Joy Unspeakable
>    is not silent,
> it moans, hums, and bends
> to the rhythm of a dancing universe.
> It is a fractal of transcendent hope,
> a hologram of God's heart,
> a black hole of unknowing.
>
> . . . . . . . . . . . . . . . . . . . . . . .

---

[21] Hall, *How My Mind Has Changed*, 35.
[22] Ibid., 37.

For Africans in bondage
in the Americas
joy unspeakable is that moment of
mystical encounter
when God tiptoes into the hush arbor,
testifies about Divine suffering,
and whispers in our ears,
　"Don't forget,
　I taught you how to fly
　on a wing and a prayer,
　　when you're ready
　　　let's go!"[23]

## Lament and Relation

The organizing focus of a spirituality of tears is *lament,* a word that has biblical, theological, and pastoral meaning and significance. I construct lament as fundamentally relational. Lament is deep relation among the broken and bent. Lament is the art of life-in-relation amid both the blatant and subtle clutches of life-the-way-it-really-is. Attention to lament, then, is less about pastoral care, less about care for struggling members of the flock. Lament is more about how the flock, embedded in life-the-way-it-really-is, gathers for one another, and how such a convivial spirit blesses the world. Pastoral care attends to those who mourn. Lament is the passion that emerges between the mournful. Lament is born in the space between.

Lament is more and different from the solitary wailing walls to which we bring our sorrow, suffering, and trauma. By wailing wall I mean my early morning walks around the pond down the street

---

[23] Barbara A. Holmes, *Joy Unspeakable: Contemplative Practices of the Black Church* (Minneapolis: Fortress Press, 2017), xvii.

several years ago. There, my less-constrained howls helped me better accompany Victoria through cancer. By lament, I mean Victoria and me talking together after my walks. In this conversational space our anxiety was eased enough to bring our fears into conversation. Such conversation was our way to go on together.[24] Lament's parish home might be an ordinary Wednesday morning bible study or the lingering of two choir members in the parking lot after choir practice Wednesday night.

## Lament as Inquiry: Yes and No Days

When I was multifaith chaplain of a small liberal arts college, Victoria and I hosted dinners in our home for students, faculty, and staff. Folks from various religious orientations and no religious affiliation came for supper, twenty to forty at a time. We'd begin by holding hands in silence around the dinner table. People were invited to break the silence with one of two words, either yes or no, or with a combination of yes and no, with brief commentary on their choice. *Yes* meant a great day; *no* meant a bad day. *Yes-no* meant a more-good-than-bad-day; *no-yes* meant a more-bad-than-good day.

There were few clear *yes* or *no* days. Mostly combos. *No-yes*: "My grandfather's got to have yet another surgery. I called my mom to find out more. We are both really scared." *Yes-no*: "I called my dad

---

[24] "Go on together" and "going on together" are phrases used in postmodern psychology and psychotherapy to represent Ludwig Wittgenstein's understanding of words as the apparatus of relation. Words are the way we go on together. Postmodern theorists Tom Andersen and Harlene Anderson place words in the broader context of embodied *utterances* for the purpose of relational collaboration—words being one of the many ways, and not necessarily the dominant way, we go on together. For example, sometimes I catch myself leaning into a conversation partner's emerging expression. I discover that I am on the edge of my chair. Likewise, tears are an utterance.

to tell him that one semester of premed is enough for me. He didn't have a heart attack!" During the meal smaller groups formed where offerings around the table were expanded and nuanced in what my colleague and I called grace notes.

## A No-Yes Afternoon

As I write just now, it is late Saturday afternoon. It's a *no-yes* day. A mild melancholia creates greater desire to gather for Eucharist tomorrow morning. I imagine the *yes* and *no* experiences parishioners will bring silently to worship and offer at the altar. I would love it if the *no-yes* folks could somehow find one another after worship. What stories might we tell, and what might emerge in the sharing of them?

## A Yes-No Community

I live in one of the poorer counties of Maine. Local churches offer a lot of people power to help sustain those who are at or over the edge. One parish offers a warming center during the cold months. Between fifty and one hundred people show up for lunch and bags of food. Over time, more sufficient people from the community come out of a hunger for community. The distinction between server and served dissolves.

Four or five people from the parish prepare and serve the meal. They've shared kitchen duty for several years. Within the group, life-the-way-it-really-is manifests as cancer, divorce, incarceration, domestic violence, addiction, dementia, infidelity, child sexual abuse, homelessness, and more. They lightly hold one another's brokenness. Sorrow, suffering, and trauma are shared through the utterances of conversation, laughter, tears, cooking, serving, and cleaning up. Time at the warming center, both in the kitchen and around the tables, slows down for relation.

## Lament and the Self

Relation with self, too, is lamentational. Our internal dialogue is polyphonic. Sometimes our inner voices are in rhythm and on pitch. Sometimes they compete for attention. Voices internalized from earlier trauma and suffering, often manifested as shame, guilt, righteousness, belittlement, or inadequacy, drown out gentler and kinder voices. Voices from our culture, which makes sacrosanct the sufficient self, seep into and muddle the voices of connection. At times, experience collars us, reveals sufficiency's hold on us, and slows us down to tune our inner voices in the service of a more relational symphony of the self.

Back in the day, I served as chaplain in an inpatient hospice facility in the Boston area. Ben was a patient with whom I was particularly close. He was a lively one, from my region of the South, who spent many of his early years as a hobo, and liked to remind me that his theme song was "My Way." Ben died while I was visiting other patients down the hall. I did not get word of his death. I walked into Ben's room expecting to pick up where we left off.

The stillness of death.[25] No need to write down the time the visit started and ended. No need to deliver a presence that lightened his load. No need to chart the encounter in a way that ensured reimbursement. No need to be a sufficient chaplain by means of an efficient stewarding of the visit and the day. For a long moment I stood there not just as a chaplain but as his friend. I saw Ben,

---

[25] I have seen many dead bodies. Yet Ben's body, that morning, was uniquely unnerving. As I reflect now on the experience, the painting of *The Body of the Dead Christ in the Tomb* by Hans Holbein the Younger, painted between 1520 and 1522, comes to mind. I find that the painting penetrates the filters we use to absorb death, and I find that my contemplation of the painting exposes the impermanence of life in a way that loosens and dissolves, for a while, our priorities that are in the service of sufficiency.

the quilt on his bed, the photographs on the bedside table, and his toothbrush in the bathroom, all with an attention I hadn't had before. How much do I miss by crossing the thresholds of the dying as one with a role to fill and a good to deliver? What do I not see with the prescription lens of professional chaplain? Where might a curiosity borne in the territory of the moment, glasses off, move our conversations?

## Teachers of Lament

Most of our teachers for the formation of a more lamentational Christian community, whom we will meet in the pages ahead, are further away from the sufficiency most of us depend on. Those whose lives are barely sustainable without intense and ongoing interdependent relation have a lot to teach us about the power of lament. Two communities stand out. One I witnessed as a child and studied and taught as an adult: the Student Nonviolent Coordinating Committee (SNCC). The other I served among for several years: the patients, families, and caretakers of the first wave of the AIDS pandemic, often referenced as the Missing Generation.

SNCC was organized after the student lunch counter protests in the early 1960s of the civil rights movement in the southern United States. It was a community of mostly younger black men and women from the South along with mostly white, college-aged students from other parts of the country. They joined together to take up the very dangerous work of voter registration in the rural Deep South.

The sustenance for their daily expense of selves was early morning coffee on the porches of the sharecroppers they sought to empower and late nights of animated conversation among themselves. Imagine a rising senior at Syracuse University and Kwame Ture (Stokely Carmichael before he changed his name) debating the violence or nonviolence of SNCC's strategies. United States Representative John Lewis, one-time chairperson of SNCC, remembers the rousing and absorbing conversations with fellow "Snickers" (a nickname given to members of SNCC) as the enactment of SNCC's "business plan."[26]

The business plan required and depended on intense relation. White students were trained for the 1964 Mississippi Freedom Summer at what was then Western College in Oxford, Ohio. The night before they were bused to Mississippi, they received news, at the closing assembly, that three civil rights worker—Andrew Goodman, Michael Schwerner, and James Chaney—had gone missing after being stopped for a "traffic violation" after leaving a meeting with black church members whose building had been burned to the ground. Three days later their burned-out car was found. Two months later their bodies were discovered buried under an earthen dam, each having been shot in the head at point-blank range. Deep and ongoing lamentational relation helped to ease deep fears, strengthened fierce resolve, and stoked the passion of SNCC volunteers.

The Missing Generation is the 235,000 people in the United States who died of AIDS between 1982 and 1993, before AIDS became a more chronic illness. I served among the Missing Generation between 1985 and 1993. Among its members I witnessed an illogical power issuing from weakness shared, a restorative force that burrowed up and through what was a seemingly impenetrable granite of horrific death and a nation that mostly abandoned and judged them. Their tears-in-relation hydrated an arid landscape of death, bigotry, and neglect. Their shared sorrow created and sustained hope.

---

[26] The Rev. John Lewis used the phrase "business plan" in his keynote address to the SNCC fiftieth anniversary conference at Shaw University, Raleigh, North Carolina, April 15–18, 2010.

Linda, who made her way from the streets to our parish, slowly garnered the courage to take Eucharist and from Eucharist to engage in parish life. And the survivors of the 1994 Rwandan genocide make us more aware of the power of rituals of lament when hope seems impossible. They reveal the almost unimaginable possibility of forgiveness through processes of lament. Present-day social movements such as Black Lives Matter and #MeToo herald a new awakening of the power of communal lament after several quieter decades.

## A Skin in the Game

My passion for ministry among sorrowful, suffering, and traumatized persons and communities stems from my early years in Albany, Georgia. I was raised in a violent home, where my mother and siblings suffered many manifestations of abuse. The trauma of our home remains a disruptive, embodied, relational, and lasting spiritual crisis that requires regular prayerful attention and lamentational conversation. I also witnessed public violence on the sidewalk in front of my father's clothing store on Broad Avenue in downtown Albany. Broad Avenue was the major scene of the Albany movement, which lasted from October 1961 to August 1962. It is considered one of the most vicious chapters of the civil rights movement, and is recognized as the movement's first big failure in terms of progress made toward desegregation. Lessons learned from the Albany movement contributed to the success of the Birmingham campaign, which followed shortly thereafter.

I was ten at the time of the Albany Movement. I was exposed to large protests met with police on foot and on horseback, with shields and helmets, attack dogs, and fire hoses. Protesters—children included—were thrown into paddy wagons. Until we moved from Albany in 1965, I witnessed the unhinged bigotry of adults close to me, who otherwise offered spaces safer than my home in which to learn and relate. I was disturbed and confused by the contradiction. For example, I remember the vitriol of a seventh-grade teacher, who often fumed about Dr. King and rambled on about membership in the KKK. And I remember my dad's best friend, who came into my dad's store when the assassination of President Kennedy was announced on the radio. He shouted, "They finally got that nigger lover."

The domestic and public terror of Albany arouses and sustains my vocation-long desire and commitment to build bridges between the pastor's study and the public square. This book is one such bridge.

The construction of lament, which unfolds in the following chapters, bears an asterisk. My voice is conditioned by my positionality. I write as a straight, white, middle-class, educated man and Episcopal priest who, through such privilege, composes at a great distance from those whom I write about—the sorrowful, suffering, and traumatized. At times, I will not see as clearly as those who are closer to the "open wound of life in this world."[27] I pray that, in the balance, my writing expresses more respectful curiosity than asserted knowledge.

## My Hope for Readers

First, I hope to inspire us to review our own lives, parishes, and communities to determine if there are active lamentational relations and conversations going on. If not, how might we create them? If so, how are we stewarding them? How might we fashion new ones?

We cannot fathom what pain parishioners bring into Sunday worship, what's inside the prayerful reflections of many who kneel after communion, what's behind the smiles at the sharing of the

---

[27] Jürgen Moltmann, *The Trinity and the Kingdom* (Minneapolis: Fortress Press, 1993), 49.

peace. We can, however, imagine and offer safer spaces for them to converse with one another about what is going on and what matters.

Over time, here and there, as we imagine and implement these safer spaces for lamentational relations and conversation, the veneer of sufficiency that we wear to church peels away and the hardwood of the body of Christ is more fully experienced. Flannery O'Connor, in the short story "Revelation," writes:

> A visionary light settled in her eyes. She saw the streak as a vast swinging bridge extending upward from the earth through a field of living fire. Upon it a vast horde of souls were rumbling toward heaven. There were whole companies of white trash, clean for the first time in their whole lives, and hordes of black niggers in white robes, and battalions of freaks and lunatics shouting and clapping and leaping like frogs. And bringing up the end was a tribe of people whom she recognized at once as those who, like herself and Claud, had always had a little of everything and the God-given wit to use it right. She leaned forward to observe them closer. They were marching behind the others with great dignity, accountable as they had always been for good order and common sense and respectable behavior. They alone were on key. Yet you could see by their shocked and altered faces that even their virtues were being burned away.[28]

Second, I hope readers discover that making and populating safer spaces for lamentational conversation in the parish setting is a contemplative act. By *contemplation,* I do not mean another way to pray, or the next new way to get to God. Conversation slows us down and brings into clearer focus what is going on in the circle

---

[28] Flannery O'Connor, "Revelation," in *The Complete Stories* (New York: Farrar, Straus and Giroux, 1946), 508.

of relation *now*, the eternal moment where God waits for us. By *moment,* I mean a curious, kindly, respectful examination of what is presently happening with us and our relations with respect to what is required of us, what we desire, value, and prefer for our lives-in-relation. Contemplation, I find, is the full-bodied, open-hearted attention to the moment. How we get to the moment is the contemplative act. Yesterday afternoon my Anglican prayer beads took me to the moment; this morning Bach Cantata 180, *Adorn Yourself, Dear Soul*. Later in the book we will learn about less "sufficient" contemplative practice, what Barbara Holmes names crisis contemplation.

Prayerful attention to the forever available *now* brings into greater focus the wounded self, neighbor, and world. It helps expose our hurried, anxious, often unwitting, automatic clamoring for sufficiency, a clamoring that leads us to shelter ourselves from, anesthetize, and throw our pain at others. We learn that our histories with hurt and trauma are not anachronistic, "back there." Rather, they are embodied and yearn for engagement and healing.[29] Prayerful attention to the moment, personal and corporate, is "divine therapy, the perennial clearinghouse of the soul, a deliberate detachment from the tyranny of emotions, the addiction to self-image, and the false promises of the world."[30]

Moreover, the eternally present moment breaks the tyranny of the past and future, which overdetermines persons and communities for sufficiency's sake. We are released, for a time, from what might

---

[29] Recent research elucidates how trauma from the past is embodied in the present. Trauma "re-wires" our brain and manifests in ways that negatively affect our daily lives and relations. See Bessel Van Der Kolk, *The Body Keeps the Score: Brain, Mind, and Body in the Healing of Trauma* (New York: Penguin Books, 2015).

[30] Citation from the Center for Action and Contemplation newsletter, *The Mendicant* 8, no. 2 (Spring 2018): 1.

have been and what could be. As Paul Tillich reminds us, the past and future are ours to place in God.[31] With our burden lightened, we may rest in love. At rest, our lives-the-way-they-really-are are more vulnerable to and open for God. From rest, we depart in greater solidarity with God, hungrier for company with one another and our desperately hurting world.

Third, and most important for me, I hope readers refresh and embrace their citizenship in the society of the fragile and resilient. An enlivened civility exposes a patch of the church's underbelly, our noblesse oblige inclination "to help those in need."

Prayerful questions arise. How do we serve without succumbing to the disposition of sufficient ones sacrificing for the less sufficient others? How do we stand down sanctification's relentless attempt to bend our desire to care into a duty to serve? Some of the words of James Baldwin, thoughts about the plight of his people, come to mind:

> This past, the Negro's past . . . this endless struggle to achieve and reveal and confirm a human identity . . . contains for all its horror, something very beautiful. I do not mean to be sentimental about suffering . . . but people who cannot suffer can never grow up, can never discover who they are.[32]

Civility in the society of the fragile and resilient ones is inquiry about, engagement with, and risky embodiment of what we confess and trust to be human, and a call to discover greater dimensions of our humanity.

---

[31] Paul Tillich, *The Eternal Now* (New York: Charles Scribner's Sons, 1963), chap. 11.

[32] Baldwin, *The Fire Next Time*, 98.

## What's Ahead

The book is divided into two parts. In Part I, "Coming Together," I elucidate the relational heart of lament, touching on lament's biblical, theological, psychological, and social dimensions. Part II, "Going on Together," focuses on the application of the art of lament in the contexts of parishes and the broader Christian community.

## Part I

# Coming Together

*The LORD sets the prisoners free;
the LORD opens the eyes of the blind;
The LORD lifts up those who are bowed down.*

—PSALM 146:7

*R*ecently, at a meeting of a men's spirituality group, during the silence before we completed our time together, I had an image of a treatment room at the Spalding Rehabilitation Hospital in Boston. An elderly man was learning to walk again. His hands held tightly to the two wooden beams between which he was situated. He pulled himself along slowly, one short movement forward at a time. Movement-rest-movement-rest.

His laborious but determined efforts to walk were analogous to the rhythm and tone of our men's meeting. We pulled ourselves along, one story to the next. One of us had just survived a car wreck in which he easily could have been killed. Another, a day or two before, had chatted with a prisoner who was about to be released, asking him, "What do you imagine for your life when you leave here?" Another shared how serious illness, his and his wife's, had slowed them down, yet anxiety visited less frequently and did not stay as long and gratitude visited more frequently and stayed longer. He said, "I think I am a better priest." Another shared a conversation he had had with his mother, who was suffering from Alzheimer's—it was the last time she knew him as her son. Another recalled a recent conversation with a combat soldier who reflected on killing people. Another talked about how his priesthood was something of a forty-year quest to work out his own salvation.

What does our men's spirituality group meeting say about God? This is the question we seek to answer in Part I. In Chapter 1 we rethink the nature of grief and grief's relation to lament. In Chapter 2 we carefully construct the five-phase trajectory of lament—wailing-lament-solidarity-joy-justice. In Chapter 3 we ask what the cross teaches us about lament. In Chapter 4 we pray to God as an image of lament in Christian community.

# 1

# Toward Sadness

## *The Arc of Grief*

Every few years I make a retreat at Christ in the Desert Monastery in the high desert of New Mexico. The monks and guests gather to pray at roughly 4:00, 6:00, and 7:00 a.m.; at noon; and at 3:00, 6:00, and 9:00 p.m. The first couple of days the tolling of the bell at 3:50 a.m. to announce the first canonical hour is startling, and I have to force myself to get up. After a few days the sound becomes more of a gentle summons.

I am beckoned to sadness. The daily office is an ancient ritual that slowly opens my heart to the terrors of the world and the tremors of my life. The terror of children starving in Yemen. The tremor of my mother moving more deeply into end-stage Alzheimer's.

Over time I have learned to welcome the sadness that comes with praying the hours. For me, the converse of sadness is not happiness; it is despair, the stale sadness that comes with our abject and covert attempts to dodge and outrun life-the-way-it-really-is, our daily quest to blunt existence.

I open my heart to existence and my heart breaks. Sadness. I close my heart to existence and my heart calcifies. Depression. Most days I move between open and closed, tears and shouts.

Sadness is more than that which comes upon us, more than what we go through. I continue to learn, and trust, that sadness is an intentional way to live in the light of Christ. Sadness is something like a liturgy of the hours. Sadness is our means for making space for regular pauses, silences, and exchanges, exercises that keep the heart open in what some call the hurricane of life.

Take, for instance, last Thursday morning at 5:16 am. Shall I kneel at the feet of the current horror that is Yemen or push Yemen out of my consciousness by means of distraction? Like losing myself in the online *New York Times*. If I had chosen to make my way through the opinion page, a spurned sadness might manifest as anxiety, sneak up on me later in the day, taunting me in subtle ways. Out of nowhere I might bark at existence. Woe to the telemarketer who calls offering an easier way to pay off student loans I no longer have.

### Grief Is Prelude to Lament

Grief, as mentioned in the Introduction, is a contemplative praying, an opening of the heart to life-the-way-it-really-is. Psychologist Thomas Attig reminds us that "grieving involves nothing less than relearning the world of our experience."[1] When grieving and aggrieved persons bring their sorrow, suffering, and trauma into intentionally constructed and serendipitously discovered community, lamentational relation is established. A church offers a group experience for those who are suffering losses or sponsors a trauma-sensitive yoga class in its basement. An older, transgendering person, who looks for and finds an affirming church, has a chance encounter at coffee hour with a younger person who has recently come

---

[1] Thomas Attig, "Relearning the World: Making Meaning and Finding Meaning," in *Meaning Reconstruction and the Experience of Loss*, ed. Robert Neimeyer (Washington, DC: The American Psychological Association, 2000), 33.

out as gay. They have a lot to talk about. The younger person ends up driving the older person to appointments at the VA hospital.

## Narrative Surrender

Sociologist Arthur Frank tells us much about narrative surrender. The transformation of personal grief to relational lament is compromised by two dominant cultural narratives. First, our experiences of sorrow, suffering, and trauma are colonized by professional experts, organized into a "unifying general view,"[2] replete with diagnostic categories and translated into the language of illness. Our now-scrubbed-down stories are handed back to us. They inform and instruct us and our loved ones about what's going on and what needs to be done about it. Our unwashed stories are now secondary, alternative accounts.[3] Frank writes, "Folk no longer go to bed and die, cared for by family and neighbors who have a talent for healing. Folk go to paid professionals who reinterpret their pain as symptoms, using a language that is unfamiliar and overwhelming."[4] In contrast, as congregations make conversational space for the sorrowful, suffering, and traumatized to be heard, something more than venting takes place. Their stories are being handed back to them *in their own words*. Colloquial discourse helps redeem colonized pain.

As mentioned in the Introduction, it took Ben's dead body to release me, for a time, from the colonization of my pastoral authority by hospice standards of care. Over time I discovered that my effectiveness as a hospice chaplain was related to how lightly I held the standards. To hold lightly meant to offer a presence that

---

[2] Arthur W. Frank, *The Wounded Storyteller* (Chicago: University of Chicago Press, 1995, 2013), 13.

[3] Ibid., 7.

[4] Ibid., 5.

turned expertise upside down. I worked hard to stay in a learning, curious position. I worked at offering a presence that opened space for patients and their loved ones to take back and take hold of experiences that had been rewritten by modern medicine.

In the second dominant cultural narrative we are coached to express feelings as a way to get through and over the violations, abuses, isolations, losses, and transitions of life-the-way-it-really-is. Grief has become work, something we need to "get out" and "work through." We are encouraged to exorcize anger, sadness, frustration, yearning, numbness, despair, confusion, and hopelessness. And, if we don't purge fast enough, we are made to wonder if we are psychological and spiritual malingerers. The latest edition of the American Psychiatric Association's *Diagnostic and Statistical Manual of Mental Disorders (DSM-5)* determines that if we don't have it together within six months after a traumatic event, we may suffer from "persistent complex bereavement disorder." Sadness has been "medicalized." Too little respect and attention are paid to what Thomas à Kempis called the proper sorrows of the soul to which the psalmist summons us: "The sacrifice acceptable to God is a broken spirit" (Ps 51:17a).

The following two stories illustrate our culture's approach to grief.

## Narrative Reclamation

Nicole, a middle-aged woman, came for counseling at the advice of healthcare providers. They believed Nicole was suffering, in part, from complicated grief due to the death of her husband, Danny, three years earlier. The providers thought Nicole's anxiety, headaches, occasional numbness and tingling in her face, trouble getting words out, and belligerent attitude toward them might be part of an acute grief response.

During our first few meetings there were three voices in the room: Nicole's, the present-in-spirit and at times dominant health-care providers' chorus of "complicated grief," and mine. As we continued to meet, Nicole's story of the love of her life dying and her fierce resolve to give him the best death possible soon quieted and later dissolved the thin narrative of the health profession's sense of Nicole's journey.

The diagnosis about which Nicole and I were curious, and which we began to tentatively hold, was post-traumatic stress disorder (PTSD). The sudden discovery of Danny's brain cancer and Nicole's continuous efforts to alleviate the quick and excruciatingly painful death Danny suffered left Nicole terrorized and depleted.

The story of Nicole's last three years is not failure to thrive or a struggle to get over and move along after her husband's death. Rather, Nicole's story is one of courage, a story of a spouse's valiant commitment to gift her husband with as peaceful a death as possible. The story presently emerging from her loss is a determination to reconstruct a life turned upside-down, leaving her heart, finances, and social network in disarray.

And what of the physical and attitude problems that the health-care system used to objectify Nicole as possibly wrestling with complicated grief? Nicole and I saw the wisdom in a second diagnosis from clinicians in the nearest teaching hospital; she is presently recovering from brain surgery to treat trigeminal neuralgia.

I do not mean to degrade or place blame on Nicole's healthcare providers. They cared for Nicole as best they could under challenging conditions. The soldiers of modern medicine march to the sound of a *restitution narrative*.[5] When healing fails, the response is to try harder. The harder the soldiers work to find out what's possibly wrong and what might work, the less time and patience are

---

[5] The structure and stature of the restitution narrative is richly developed by Arthur Frank. See ibid., 75–96.

taken to listen to the voice of those they treat. Studies indicate that the patient's voice carries a vital wisdom toward healing; however, research and continuing education about the value of patients' expression and authority do not routinely permeate the more cloistered terrain of the treatment room. In that room the caregiver's eye contact often is primarily with the computer screen. The patient's face, often off to the side, is only intermittently attended to. Nonverbal signals in particular are thus likely to be missed.

Furthermore, my county in Maine is rural and poor. There are not nearly enough physicians and allied caregivers to care effectively for those in their charge. Recently I ran into a former student of mine, now a nurse practitioner, who works in a clinic for the marginalized and underserved. She said: "I can't believe I've been doing this for six years. It feels like six hundred years." Under such circumstances, there is the temptation, and at times a demand, to rush to judgment, to settle on quick diagnosis. Problems that develop between scheduled visits most often are addressed in the emergency room.

Also, rural areas are populated with poorer people, who are less likely to be listened to by those who care for them.[6] I learned from my experience caring for poorer people at Grady Hospital that I had to work harder to be fully present with those of social locations different from mine. I witnessed how easy it is for well-intended caregivers to unknowingly become part of the system that silences, in subtle and not so subtle ways, poorer people, people of color, immigrants, people with HIV/AIDS, and others who are vulnerable.[7] When patients with fewer teeth, oily hair, and a crying

---

[6] "6 Charts That Illustrate the Divide between Rural and Urban America," PBS News Hour, March 17, 2017, available online.

[7] See Laura Skopec and Sharon K. Long, "Poor Treatment by Health Care Providers and Staff Is More Common among Vulnerable Populations," *Health Reform Monitoring Survey* by the Urban Institute Health Policy Center (October 24, 2016).

baby at their feet speak up and advocate for themselves and their loved ones, they are more likely to be objectified as offensive and catalogued as troublemakers. They are easier to erase. My courage to critique the healthcare system's care of poor and marginalized people comes from having learned from my mistakes.

Nicole, because she was not poor, had greater agency to agitate; she was thus less at risk when she "demanded to speak rather than be spoken for and to represent [herself] rather than being represented or, in the worst cases, rather than be effaced entirely."[8] Nicole had the wherewithal to use counseling to reclaim and declare a personhood that had been objectified by the entries in her medical chart.

## Slow Down

Mary came for counseling because her best friend, Sean, had died suddenly a month before. Between our second and third meetings Mary attended Sean's memorial service. During our third meeting Mary said that she felt better. She noted that she was quickly moving through Elisabeth Kübler-Ross's five stages of grief, and that she felt ready to get on with life.

Mary's haste reminded me of words psychologist Harry Goolishian often shared with his trainees: "If you want to get somewhere fast, you must proceed slowly." I offered Mary the opportunity to slow down. I suggested to Mary that Sean, new to death, might need and certainly desire for her to hang out a bit longer. I shared that death can be lonely. And, in many cultures and religions, the dead need our help to cross over into the fullness of the light. Mary looked bemused.

In our previous meetings I had learned that Sean had been for Mary what she called a "deep listener." Mary trusted and sometimes

---

[8] Frank, *The Wounded Storyteller,* 13.

depended on Sean's wisdom. I attended to Mary's puzzled expression by suggesting that we invite Sean to sit with us for a meeting or two, so that she and Sean could help each other move along.

## Continuing Bonds

Emerging grief research equips and inspires healers to attend to an ongoing relational space in which the bereft and deceased nurture and sustain a continuing bond on the way to new life.[9] Stewarding the bond is more than a counterpoint to the cultural narrative of getting on with life after a loss. Rather, attention is given to the possibility of loosening the grip on what was, so that the bereft and deceased may go on together toward what is and will be their continuing conversational partnership. Together they attend to a relational space in which they discover perspective, strength, direction, reconciliation, and blessing.

I sometimes share with persons who come for counseling the practice of letter writing with deceased persons who have been a formative presence in their lives.[10] I invite the person to "transcribe" a letter, say, from a beloved aunt, about a particular situation the person is struggling with. Often the person responds, "You mean you want me to write a letter to Aunt Jane?" I might say, "No, Aunt Jane wants to write you. She has things she wants to say. She needs a scribe. Give it a shot. Bring the letter along next week. I am curious about what we might learn from her."

Karen has been entangled in a hurtful relation with her sisters. Her brother, Mike, who died of cancer twenty years ago, was her best friend. Now Mike's daughter, Brenda, is getting married. Karen is anguished about attending the wedding for a number of

---

[9] See Dennis Klass, Steven L. Nickman, and Phyllis R. Silverman, eds., *Continuing Bonds: New Understandings of Grief* (Oxford, UK: Taylor and Francis, 1996).

[10] I am grateful to family therapists Peggy Penn, PhD, and Marty Roberts, PhD, for introducing me to the practice of letter writing in the voice of the deceased.

reasons, especially that she will be in close proximity to her sisters and ex-husband Ben. I encourage her to try the practice of being Mike's scribe.

In the letter that Karen writes, Mike remains the good brother he has always been:

Dear Karen,

I miss you. I miss our friendship and your company. I would like to be by Brenda's side to walk her down the aisle. I am sorry Ben was invited, but this is our family. Ignore him and let go of the past. Have fun for me, celebrate for both of us, and let Brenda know how much the family loves her. The family issues should not affect the love we have for Brenda and the joy we share at her wedding. Don't let your sisters bring you down.

I want you to be happy and have fun. You watched over Brenda in my absence. Thank you. Even though she acts like she doesn't need it, keep giving her love. I will be there with both of you on that day, as I was with you on your wedding day.

Our relationship was special and rare. Something we both appreciated. I wish everyone could join in the camaraderie. Don't let their criticism bring you down.

It is sad the family is so fractured now. The wedding can be a place to mend the problems. If not, have fun and be true to yourself. Their problems are not yours, so don't get sucked in. Enjoy yourself with me.

Love, Mike.

James shares letters with his father, who died several years ago. James mentioned that his father has yet to write him about a present struggle, one his father knows is new territory for James. James noted that his father is still wrestling with his thoughts about the situation. James anticipates his father's reply, aware that his father takes time to reflect on new situations. The father's time out to consider the matter expresses the lively and evolving bond James and his father share.

Uncle Mitchell was a father figure to me. He helped me through bad times regarding my family of origin. I often think *WWMD*—what would Mitchell do in this or that situation. My ruminations, as meaningful as they are, juxtapose past experiences with Mitchell onto situations in my present life. I have some dictation to catch up on.

Cynthia, a social worker and incest survivor, many years ago created support groups for victims of incest. Of late, Cynthia has been reflecting on the many members of the support groups who suicided:

> I want to tell you about a dream I had last night where I made a quilt in honor of a friend who had died. I awoke with a thought to make a quilt in honor of my friends from SIS [Support for Incest Survivors]. So, I have begun to design it this morning. It will probably take me a while to make it.

Imagine letters Cynthia might receive from her friends in response to the quilt sewn in their honor. Imagine letters Holocaust victims Anne Frank and Etty Hillesum[11] might write to those who lost loved ones in the terrorist attack at Tree of Life Synagogue in Pittsburgh on October 27, 2018. Imagine letters Emmett Till might have written to his mother, Mrs. Mamie Till-Mobley, about his tortured death. What might he have said to his mother in regard to her decision to have an open casket? Would he honor a decision

---

[11] The diaries of Etty Hillesum, not as widely known as the diary of Anne Frank, are compelling. See *An Interrupted Life: The Diaries of Etty Hillesum 1941–1943* (New York: Pantheon Books, 1983).

that changed the course of the civil rights movement for the good? I like to imagine that he "Amen-ed!" the decision and her will "to keep on keeping on" for the sake of the movement.

## Catharsis Reexamined

*Catharsis* is generally understood in our culture as purgation in the service of moving on. This understanding of catharsis is a thin description of grief. Michael White, cofounder of narrative therapy, revives the original Greek notion of catharsis. He suggests that "the original meaning has less to do with purgation and more to do with collectively moving people from one place to another in an experience of transformation."[12] Catharsis is the movement from despair to sadness to hope.

Both individual and communal lament psalms are cathartic in the classic sense. The trajectory is transformational, an emancipatory movement that mirrors the journey of Holy Week. For instance, Psalm 74 foreshadows Maundy Thursday's angst:

> O God, why do you cast us off forever? (v. 1)

Good Friday's horror:

> They set your sanctuary on fire;
>     they desecrated the dwelling places of your
>         name,
>     bringing it to the ground. (v. 7)

Holy Saturday's harrowing of hell:

---

[12] Michael White, *Reflection on Narrative Practice* (Adelaide, South Australia: Dulwich Center Publications, 2000), in Lynn Hoffman, *Family Therapy: An Intimate History* (New York: W. W. Norton and Company, 2002), 256.

> Yet God my King is from of old,
>> working salvation in the earth. (v. 12)

and Easter morning's cosmic victory:

> You have fixed all the bounds of the earth;
>> you made summer and winter.
>>> (v. 17)

We see a similar trajectory in Psalm 13:

> How long, O Lord? Will you forget me forever?
>> (v. 1a)

> Consider and answer me, O Lord my God;
>> give light to my eyes or I will sleep the sleep
>> of death. (v. 3)

> But I trusted in your steadfast love;
>> my heart shall rejoice in your salvation. (v. 5)

> I will sing to the Lord,
>> because he has dealt bountifully with me.
>>> (v. 6)

And in Psalm 55:

> Give ear to my prayer, O God;
>> do not hide yourself from my supplication.
>>> (v. 1)

> Fear and trembling come upon me, and horror
>> overwhelms me. (v. 5)

Cast your burden on the LORD,
    and he will sustain you;
he will never permit
    the righteous to be moved. (v. 22)

But you, O God, will cast them down
    into the lowest pit;
the bloodthirsty and treacherous
    shall not live out half their days.
But I will trust in you. (v. 23)

## Desegregating Lament Psalms

In the liturgy the lament psalms are mostly relocated to burial rites, the penitential seasons, and Holy Week. As such, we are drawn more to the first part of the psalms, the Maundy Thursday and Good Friday dynamic: "I know how that feels." "That's my experience." "God knows the trouble I've seen." The experience is more about identification than redemption. The Holy Saturday and Easter movements in the latter part of the psalms seem out of season.

When I recite the lament psalms in the penitential seasons, I am likely to lose focus when the good news comes along. "Hey, may I wallow a bit longer please? It's not Easter yet!" When we lasso the lament psalms and corral them into the "sad" seasons, we dissolve the deliverance arc of the lament psalms into a despair-hope duality.

But as we find ways to free the lament psalms from the liturgical calendar and integrate them into our ongoing life together, this despair-hope duality begins to loosen. A trajectory starts to coalesce, and the pain and struggles of life are more normalized. Parishioners desire to bring more of the lived experience of sorrow, suffering, and trauma into the community discourse. The parish discourse creates resolve to work toward greater possibilities for healing and hope. Parishes discover new perspectives on and enthusiasm for ministry and mission that flow more from solidarity and less from duty. Parishes become more curious about the liberative movements and martyrdoms of the Christian tradition; a greater kinship with the saints and martyrs is established. Parishes discover hidden and new knowledge and skills, flowing from convivial engagement, for making a difference for the good. They stretch their imaginations as to directions for and steps toward the future.[13] Lament psalms engage parishioners and empower parishes better to bless one another and the world.

## Psalmic Fire

Moreover, a more psalmic[14] dynamic of despair and hope equips congregations to recognize their lamentational kinship with social movements that express the cathartic arc of despair-sadness-hope.[15] Catharsis as transformation is mirrored in the fight songs of the civil rights movement.

> Ain't gonna let nobody
> Turn me 'round
> Turn me 'round
> Ain't gonna let nobody
> Turn me 'round
> I'm gonna keep on walkin'

---

[13] A cathartic gestalt in regard to congregational life mirrors the outcomes of cathartic conversations in narrative therapy. See Michael White, *Maps of Narrative Practice* (New York: W. W. Norton and Company, 2007), 194–96.

[14] Dorothee Sölle elaborates on the dynamic of "psalmic language" in *Suffering* (Philadelphia: Fortress Press, 1975), 70–78.

[15] The cathartic arc of despair and hope, psalmic language, is beautifully, vividly offered in particular Bach cantatas to which I regularly turn. Listen, with lyrics in hand, to Cantata 199, *My Heart Swims in Blood*, and Cantata 131, *Out of the Depths, I Call to Thee*.

Keep on talkin'
Marchin' into freedom land.

Oh, freedom!
Oh, freedom!
Oh, freedom over me!
And before I'd be a slave
I'll be buried in my grave
And go home to my Lord and be free!

If I had known what to listen for as a boy watching the protests in front of my father's store, I may have witnessed these choruses transforming the marchers' fear into fierce resolve, extraordinary courage, and unspeakable joy.

## Holy Grief

Holy grief is a slower praying of life-the-way-it-really-is. From such prayer one's own voice begins to emerge. This voice "re-claims the capacity to tell one's story as . . . halting, self-doubting, and inarticulate"[16] as it may sound in the telling. When one finds oneself stammering to communicate lived experience, something sacred is happening. The grieving and aggrieved voice, forever na-scent, always becoming, is available to and hungry for others. Our utterances are sometimes not clearly articulated and tidied up into sentences. What does happen, almost always, is the visitation of an emerging hope that lifts our feet for the next step or two toward "beautiful, beautiful Zion." Grief is being translated into lament.

In the next chapter we explore the relational dimensions of lament.

---

[16] Frank, *The Wounded Storyteller*, 7.

# 2

# Bound Together

## Lament and Relation

*We need, in every community, a group of angelic troublemakers. Our power is in our ability to make things unworkable. The only weapon we have is our bodies. And we need to tuck them in places so wheels don't turn.*

—BAYARD RUSTIN[1]

Terry Tempest Williams, in her book *Finding Beauty in a Broken World*, visits Ravinia, Italy, to learn about the art of making mosaics. She discovers that "a mosaic is a conversation between what is broken."[2]

Lament is conversation between those who are broken. Lament as *conversation* is in contrast to the established definition of lament as an *expression* of grief or sorrow. Expression suggests a more solitary,

---

[1] *Brother Outsider: The Life of Bayard Rustin*, directed by Nancy D. Kates and Bennett Singer. DVD. United States: Passion River, 2010.

[2] Terry Tempest Williams, *Finding Beauty in a Broken World* (New York: Pantheon Books, 2008), 6.

monologic act, resonant with grief as getting out, expelling sorrow, suffering, and trauma. A mosaic is made up of stones, tiles, or shards of glass in artful relation to one another. Lament is broken people in artful relation with and for one another. By artful, I mean imaginatively crafted configurations of relation that vivify the weary and illumine new ways to go on together. A mosaic invites the observer to find the right distance from the configuration in order to see the design of the fragments. Too close or too far and the pattern blurs. Lament invites the community of broken ones to step back from their lived experience just enough to name what we have to share with one another. Lament, then, is the ardent and fruitful endeavor of the grieving and the aggrieved to connect, the bone-tired ache for community.

## Wailing Is a Prelude to Lament

The biblical text most conversant with lament is Lamentations. Lamentations is "a small psalter of communal laments over Jerusalem, following its destruction by the Babylonians in 587 BCE."[3] The book expresses "with searing clarity [the] fear, grief, and despair" of those who "lost loved ones, a way of life, and material well-being."[4] See the first two verses of Lamentations:

> How lonely sits the city
>     that once was full of people!
> How like a widow she has become,
>     she that was great among the nations!
> She that was a princess among the provinces
>     has become a vassal.

---

[3] *New Oxford Annotated Bible* (New York: Oxford University Press, 1962, 1973), 991.

[4] Kathleen M. O'Connor, *Lamentations and the Tears of the World* (Maryknoll, NY: Orbis Books, 2002), 3.

> She weeps bitterly in the night,
>> with tears on her cheeks;
> among all her lovers
>> she has no one to comfort her;
> all her friends have dealt treacherously with her,
>> they have become her enemies. (Lam 1:1-2)

The howling does not let up. The loudest noise is the silence of God, a matter we address later in the chapter. The unanswered despair at the heart of Lamentations is what I call *wailing*, a pain too raw to enunciate.

My first ongoing encounter with wailing was among those of the Missing Generation, the first generation of the AIDS pandemic—those who died quick, painful deaths and those who loved and cared for them. Words could not keep up with our experience. We murmured through big loss, purred while sharing fierce love, and muttered while offering great care.

I am grateful to post-Holocaust theologian, Dorothee Sölle, whose book *Suffering* helps us pray when we are in suffering that leaves us at a loss for words, bereft of understanding, disoriented, frozen of heart and hope. She constructs suffering in three phases. "The first . . . is to find a language that leads us out of uncomprehended suffering that makes one mute."[5] The discovery and expression of the language is phase two, "an indispensable step on the way to the third, in which liberation . . . can be organized."[6]

Wailing, then, is phase one suffering, the narthex of lament. Wailing is the lived experience of Maundy Thursday's liturgical stripping of the altar during the reciting of Psalm 22, without the faint smell of Easter lilies in the wings wafting over "My God, my God, why hast thou forsaken me?" Wailing is the disquieting, isolating, inarticulate, desperate attempt of sorrowful, suffering, and

---

[5] Dorothee Sölle, *Suffering* (Philadelphia: Fortress Press, 1975), 70.
[6] Ibid., 72.

traumatized people to express their experience in a manner that can be handed over to and shared in community.

Wailing has at least three dimensions: (1) Wailing erupts now and again in each of our lives-the-way-they-really-are; (2) wailing is the noise of our cultural malaise; and (3) wailing is the ongoing and unending experience of trauma victims.

First, wailing is the clamor we all make at times. Philosopher Nicholas Wolterstorff reflects on an early attempt to write about the sudden and tragic loss of his son, Eric:

> Rather early in the process of writing I tried to join the fragments into a continuous flow, but it didn't work. My life had been fragmented, so my lament would have to be fragmented as well. I think of the white space between the fragments as silence. In the face of death, we should not talk much.[7]

Second, wailing is the din of "an officially optimistic society"[8] that relocates despair to the closet. Despair is "insidiously 'covert.' A sense of futility and hopelessness 'masquerades under the guise of well-being so pervasive as to deceive the wearers of the masks themselves.'"[9]

Sometimes our wailing is easy to spot and name. A three-year-old child wanders away from its parents before boarding a Sunday afternoon flight home from Orlando after a week at Disney World; its parents are buried in their cell phones before they have to put

---

[7] Nicholas Wolterstorff, "Grief Speaks the Truth," *The Christian Century* 136, no. 2 (January 16, 2019): 26.

[8] John Douglas Hall, "Cross and Context," *The Christian Century* 127, no. 8 (September 10, 2010): 35.

[9] The quotations from  page 90 of O'Connor's *Lamentations and the Tears of the World* are from a group of international theologians gathered at Columbia Theological Seminary to discuss the theme of hope.

them in airplane mode. Their distraction is broken by a cry they know well. As they sprint to the sound, their child flails about, panicking at their absence.

Not so easy to spot and name as wailing is a forty-five-year-old striding through the airport, adrift but not aware of it, not looking it. He or she wears an expensive business suit, wireless earbuds in, waving a phone like a baton, talking with a ghost, a subordinate back at corporate getting ready to go to a consequential meeting. There is the exciting possibility of the startup soon converting to a buyout.

But if and when it does, the itch remains. Our culture is wired to create new needs when old ones are met. The person's wailing might be embodied as chronic lower bowel syndrome, insomnia, uncontrolled anger, or an affair that is dragging on. Meanwhile, what of the spouse, who may be weaving through the week with an enduring heartache accompanied by episodic howls, restless to hear some comforting words?

Third, wailing is a dominating and undiminished language of the victims of trauma. Victims of trauma live outside the *restitution narrative* of our officially optimistic society. Numbed silence often prevails. An excerpt from a letter written by Mukangwije Lea, a survivor of the Rwandan genocide, reads:

> My primary concern, however, is still my mother. She is very old and has been through so much. If you look closely, all the people who inhabit this village are traumatized. She is in this category. She lives in a very deep silence. I try to entertain her, but you realize that she is overwhelmed with sorrow. The survivors live in a vast loneliness. This is the case with my mother, Mama Emma. Even now, she cannot fully understand what happened.[10]

---

[10] Quoted in Williams, *Finding Beauty in a Broken World*, 354.

When the sound of wailing is heard, often it is a rushed noise that tries to catch up with the experience and hog-tie it with words. The "staccato pacing of 'and then and then and then' pecks away"[11] at both the testifier and witness. The trauma "narrative is always beyond speech, and thus it is always lacking speech. [The] chaos is what can never be told; it is the hole in the telling."[12]

The challenge for those who witness the narratives of trauma victims is to be still and stay present, to resist helping them fill the hole. We are called to "hear them for all the ways in which [their testimonies] do not cohere"[13] or find resolution. We have a lot to learn from the God of Lamentations. Kathleen M. O'Connor writes beautifully of the capacity of God to stay still and present in the midst of the incessant and unrelenting wailing that is the poetry of Lamentations:

> God's speechlessness in Lamentations must be a calculated choice, a conscious theological decision, an inspired control by the book's composers, for how could a response from the deity do anything but ruin the book. No matter what God said, Lamentations would come to premature resolution, and the book's capacity to house sorrow would dissipate. Any words from God would endanger human voices. They would undercut anger and despair, foreshorten protest, and give the audience only a passing glimpse of the real terror of their condition. Divine speaking would trump all speech.[14]

---

[11] Arthur W. Frank, *The Wounded Storyteller* (Chicago: University of Chicago Press, 1995, 2013), 99.

[12] Ibid., 101–2.

[13] Shelly Rambo, *Spirit and Trauma: A Theology of Remaining* (Louisville, KY: Westminster John Knox Press, 2010), 151.

[14] O'Connor, *Lamentations and the Tears of the World*, 85.

## Characteristics of Lament

### *Lament Requires Two Voices*

Twentieth-century Russian philosopher, literary critic, and Eastern Orthodox Christian Mikail Bakhtin writes that "two voices is the minimum for life, the minimum for existence."[15] Old Testament scholar Walter Brueggemann, citing the works of Erhard Gerstenberger and Rainer Albertz, writes that the two kinds of religions in the Ancient Near East, temple- and family-based religion, come together in ancient Israel. Lament psalms, not often offered in the temple, were regularly shared in local gatherings led by lay elders to help people through times of trouble. Lament psalms were conversation starters among friends.[16] Old Testament scholar Angela Bauer, writing about our nation's fractured sense of lament in relation to 9/11, remembers Jeremiah's appeal to women to teach one another the art of leading the people in mourning:

> If the women who have led the lament are professionals, now each woman is asked to teach her female companion a dirge, both staying within their role as leaders of the mourning rituals and including the wider community of women who during wartime are the only ones left at home to join in. Indeed, the circle of addressees, who are called to carry out the command, widens to invite each and every woman as an instructor of another in their communal crying. Women across generations, regardless of family connections or any other implicit boundaries (of race and class), are learning to sing the songs of

---

[15] Quoted in Ruth Coates, *Christianity and the Exiled Author* (New York: Cambridge University Press, 1998), 167.

[16] Walter Brueggemann, "The Friday Voice of Faith," *Calvin Theological Journal* 36 (2001): 14.

mourning. Beyond discrimination, the divine imperative has become inclusive. From God through the women keeners the melody of mourning has moved to every woman.[17]

My friend Mike, following the martyrdom at Tree of Life Synagogue, reread Leon Wieseltier's *Kaddish* and shared the following excerpt:

> There has arrived from Brooklyn a new edition of the rulings of Hayyim ben Isaac of the late thirteenth century. . . . Hayyim reports on another practice in thirteenth-century Germany, of which he obviously approves: "In Speyer, it is the custom that a mourner, before the days of his mourning are over, leaves his house to join the funeral procession of another dead and to bury him, though this should [only] be done after the first three days." It would seem cruel for an individual just back from one funeral to be hustled out to another funeral; but in truth it is not cruel, it is an exercise in social responsibility. The mourner, too, has a social responsibility. His experience has conferred upon him an expertise that others need. Grief must not impede the specialist in grief. The disconsolate are the masters of consolation. They offer sympathy without illusion.[18]

Jeremiah and Hayyim ben Isaac know that stitching moan to moan creates a tapestry of hope.

### Lament Is Testimonial

Because lament is the grieving and aggrieved person's and the community's determined effort to relate with each other and others on

---

[17] Angela Bauer, "Death, Grief, Agony, and a New Creation: Re-reading Gender in Jeremiah after September 11," in *Word and World* 51, no. 2 (Fall 2002): 383.

[18] Leon Wieseltier, *Kaddish* (New York: Alfred A. Knopf, 1998), 580–81.

matters of ultimate concern, it is in the declarative voice. The blind beggar Bartimaeus shouts his way to the Lord: "When he heard that it was Jesus of Nazareth, he began to shout out and say, 'Jesus, Son of David, have mercy on me!' Many sternly ordered him to be quiet, but he cried out even more loudly, 'Son of David, have mercy on me!'" (Mk 10:47–48).

I was reminded of these verses during my time as a hospice chaplain, especially in the case of Josh, who was dying of AIDS. We met for an hour each Friday when he came to the AIDS clinic at Grady Hospital for a handful of regularly scheduled appointments. One Wednesday morning, however, Josh sought me out. He was desperate to be seen by a nurse or doctor. He was in great pain as a result of thrush, a fungal infection of the mouth, which persons with AIDS often contracted. He pleaded for help, but the clinic was already overwhelmed with patients who were suffering equally or worse. There was no room for unscheduled appointments; I could do nothing to move Josh to the front of the line. I was anxious to help, however, so after a few minutes of listening to his unrelenting demand for attention, on a whim, I told Josh to go to the office of the hospital's CEO, stand before the receptionist, and scream to high heaven about his pain. Josh wasted no time and was immediately treated. Admittedly, this was not an ideal solution, but it speaks to the power of witnessing to others when one is in pain.

There is in the human spirit an unquenchable thirst to connect, especially in times of trouble. If testifiers sense that witnesses are not understanding or attuned to their plea, they will cry more, shout louder, and search farther until they have a witness. Bartimaeus shouted over those who rebuked him. Josh stood down my sense of helplessness.

North America heralds a theology of glory that has too little patience with Bartimaeus and Josh, with lamentational testimony. The arc of worship and relations bend toward praise and thanksgiving that spring less from lamentational relation and more from obvious and insidious power relations borne of white American exceptionalism; namely, America is better than other nations, ordained by God as the true nation, and, therefore, a nation with a mission to transform the world.[19] The church's lamentational voice has been quelled.

Granted, we make a little room to wrestle with God in Lent and Holy Week, when the psalms of lament are in vogue.[20] Even then, the noise of a theology of glory hovers over and regulates our liturgical rants. We soften our protestations so that our prophetic voice is less hegemonic and more resonant with the current unabashedly jingoistic zeal of the United States. The God of emancipatory fervor has been relocated to a side chapel. Those who regularly worship there, like Bartimaeus and Josh, are objectified as troublemakers.

### Lament Requires a Witness

"Jesus stood still and said, 'Call him here'" (Mk 10:49a). Jesus then addressed Bartimaeus. A broken, contrite, and violated spirit demands more than a compassionate listener. An engaged witness moved by what is declared is required. Note the black preacher's call from the pulpit, "Do I have a witness?"

Testifier and witness take each other's hand and head for the dance floor. The choreography of the testifier-witness dance is call-response-praise, a liturgical act. The testifier calls to God for help:

> Help, O Lord, for there is no longer anyone who
>       is godly;
>    the faithful have disappeared from human-
>       kind.

---

[19] See Kelly Brown Douglas, *Stand Your Ground: Black Bodies and the Justice of God* (Maryknoll, NY: Orbis Books, 2015), 11–16.

[20] For an analysis of the church's neglect of and need for the lament psalms, see Walter Brueggemann, "The Costly Loss of Lament," *Journal of the Study of the Old Testament* 38 (1986): 57–71; and idem, "The Friday Voice of Faith," 12–21.

> They utter lies to each other;
>> with flattering lips and a double heart they
>>> speak. (Ps 12:1–2)

The testifier accuses God of absence and silence:

> O my God, I cry by day, but you do not answer;
>> and by night, but find no rest. (Ps 22:2)

The witnessing God stays put in the face of appeal and accusation; does not flee from, curb, or cut off the plaintiff's cry; and is moved to respond to the injustice:

> "Because the poor are despoiled, because the
>> needy groan,
>> I will now rise up," says the LORD;
>> "I will place them in the safety for which
>>> they long." (Ps 12:5)

The testifier's plea is transformed to praise:

> But I trusted in your steadfast love;
>> my heart shall rejoice in your salvation.
> I will sing to the LORD,
>> because he has dealt bountifully with me. (Ps
>>> 13:5–6)

### Lament Is a Relational Act in Which Testifier and Witness Are Transformed

Testifiers, in being heard to voice anew and afresh, learn from the utterances that emerge between the witnesses and themselves. Testifiers hear their testimony again as if for the first time. The witnesses, because of the relational imperative implicit in the testifiers' desire to connect and engage, are exposed, vulnerable, and, through such an encounter, changed.

As mentioned in the introduction to Part I, I remember the last time my mom knew me as her son, the last coherent conversation we had. We were sitting on the sun porch of the assisted living center watching bluebirds fly to and from their bird boxes. In a bit, after Mom answered some chatty questions, I asked her if she remembered my dad. She said that she did. After some silence I asked her if she had any good memories of him. She said that she did. After more silence she took the initiative in the conversation for the first and only time. Mom said, "Do you?" And I replied, "Do I have good memories of Dad?" She said, "Yes." I answered, "No." And Mom responded, "You should find some."

I was no longer a dutiful listener paying attention to my mother's chatter. I was the hearer of a mother's plea not to let her dead husband continue to imprison a portion of her son's heart. That exchange was Mom's appeal for all three of us to rest in peace. Mom and I left the conversation different from when we started it. Possibly, Dad did, too.

### The Testifier-Witness Dance Is a Moral Imperative for Lament

The testifier-witness dance dissolves the more fictive narrative of a testifier mostly in conversation with himself or herself, or conversing with a listener who does not have ears to hear. Because we are indoctrinated by nation and church to make smaller space for lamentational relation, the testifier often is left alone or, if luckier, with listeners offering *nonjudgmental* and *active listening/deep listening* positions. By *nonjudgmental,* I mean a non-blaming, non-critiquing, non-advising position. By *active/deep listening,* I mean a quieter, curious, prayerful attention to neighbors' distress and dilemmas. Over a few decades these positions have found nests, first in seminary pastoral care courses, then in parish care and visitation programs, and now in the general public as a way to be a good friend in times of lesser and larger struggles with life-the-way-it-really-is. In the last chapter the woman I met with shared that her friend who died was for her a deep listener. These practices have made an immense difference for the good. And yet they often fail the testifier's need for grittier engagement. Do I have a *witness?* Testifiers need witnesses who are willing and able to be drawn into the often chaotic fire of the testifier-witness dance. They need accompaniment into the abyss, not stopping at the lip. Mom demanded more from me than a son's emotional largesse. She ferociously grappled for much more, asking, "Do you?"

A college student recently came to see me for counseling for what I am slowly learning was a horrible violation. During our first visit she announced that her life slogan is, "You win some and lose most." Carefully, we are scaffolding down into the abyss. At each level I am asked to answer silently offered test questions. Are you with me? Am I going to be left down here by myself? She pleads for a witness.

Living the fictions we construct when left to ourselves, or with listeners who are more empathetic than engaging, accounts for more emaciated and burdened spirits. Left alone, the voices of shame, guilt, and futility infect our litanies of lament. These visitations make a home in our hearts. They become who we are. We can't leave the narthex of wailing to enter the sanctuary of lament.

My father regularly reminding me that I was stupid, fat, and lazy evolved into a story about myself that I have spent decades working to disprove. I have a lot of evidence to denounce the story, but the evidence weakens under the gaze of my self-scrutiny. The fiercely curious, hard-loving, enlivened interrogations of witnesses who compel me to get messier (truer) with myself and my relations break the hold, for a while, that a traumatic childhood continues to have on me.

I imagine that many of us have been haunted by relationally lacking and thereby diminishing, belittling stories about ourselves and the troubles we've seen. I imagine that we, to some degree, skirt and avoid testimony due to the shame, guilt, and futility we feel as a result of these stories. I imagine that we desire congregational and communal spaces for testifier-witness dances by which we could sweat out the relational toxins. We want to loosen the hold fictive living has on us.

If such congregational and communal spaces for the testifier-witness dance are transformational, aren't we compelled to create them? Aren't we duty bound to be agents of change at a time and in a culture that depends on a domesticated despair? In 1964, a time not unlike our present time, Thomas Merton named the moral challenge: "There is no revolution without a voice. The passion of the oppressed must first of all make itself heard at least among themselves, in spite of the insistence of the privileged oppressor that such needs cannot be real, or just, or urgent."[21]

### Lament Is a Lens through Which to Explore Salvation History

Walter Brueggemann writes that "the Bible characteristically bears witness to the formation and maintenance of human living space that is free from the pathologies of empire"—more specifically, "living space outside the totalizing regime of Pharaoh, living space outside the claims and control of the royal-priestly urban hegemony of Jerusalem."[22] Salvation history is fired in the ovens of sorrowful, suffering, and traumatized communities desperately pursuing life

---

[21] Thomas Merton, *Seeds of Destruction* (New York: Farrar, Straus and Giroux, 1964), 72.

[22] Walter Brueggemann, *Reality, Grief, Hope: Three Urgent Prophetic Tasks* (Grand Rapids, MI: Eerdmans, 2014), 147.

together beyond the reach of their oppressors. Salvation history is steeped in lament.

We are still making salvation history. Civil rights legend Fannie Lou Hamer addressed the credentials committee of the 1964 Democratic National Convention in order to persuade the convention to seat her and fellow delegates of the Mississippi Freedom Democratic Party: "I am sick and tired of being sick and tired." Lyndon Johnson, listening to the speech on television, called an impromptu press conference in order to interrupt her speech. The national television networks, on the evening news, aired the speech in protest. Fannie Lou Hamer's courageous stance was eventually rewarded—she was a delegate to the 1968 Democratic convention in Chicago. When we make salvation history, we play with dynamite—salvation history explodes "the reigning economic and political interests"[23] of the particular era in which we live.

## *Lament Is Starter Dough for More Moderate Social Movements*

Fannie Lou Hamer's speech took root, and four years later she was seated in the outer court of the tabernacle. The mainline churches,[24] in regard to lament, are indebted to those whose lamentational agitation outside the fence of the outer court helped pass more progressive social agendas. We—the mainline churches and the nation—are beneficiaries of their prophetic fire. Revolution births liberation, which births social movements, which birth policy.

---

[23] Stanley Hauerwas, "Kierkegaard and the Academy," Capps lecture, University of Virginia, October 24, 2017.

[24] By "mainline churches," I mean Protestant churches, the majority of Christians in North America. By "Protestant," I mean the Baptist, Episcopal, Lutheran, Methodist, Presbyterian, and United Church of Christ denominations. I imagine Roman Catholic parishes in many ways mirror the spirit of Protestant congregations. I do not know enough about Roman Catholic parishes to make more definitive claims about them.

Take, for instance, the marathon that was the civil rights movement of the 1950s and 1960s. A marathon is 26.22 miles. The Student Nonviolent Coordinating Committee entered around mile marker 3.2775. The Southern Christian Leadership Conference, led by Dr. King, entered around mile marker 6.555. The mainline churches did not enter the marathon until around mile marker 19.665. But every bit helps. On July 2, 1964, almost a month before the Democratic National Convention, President Johnson, with Dr. King at his side, signed the Civil Rights Act into law.

To whom are we indebted for social policies that make a difference for the good? I will cite a few. Bayard Rustin and George Houser, from the Fellowship of Reconciliation, a religious organization grounded in nonviolent resistance, were instrumental in orchestrating the 1947 Journey of Reconciliation, often acknowledged as the first freedom ride. Eight blacks and eight whites, under the auspices of the more secular CORE (Congress of Racial Equality), boarded two buses traveling from Washington, DC, through the South. Bayard Rustin was arrested in Chapel Hill, North Carolina, for refusing to leave his seat in the front of the bus. He was sentenced to a chain gang. His journal entries, made while he was serving time, were published by the *New York Post*. The publication is credited with contributing to the end of chain gangs in North Carolina. Later, Bayard Rustin, closeted by Dr. King and demonized by Adam Clayton Powell for being gay, was invited out of the closet to orchestrate the 1963 March on Washington. Why the change of heart? Marian Wright Edelman, founder of the Children's Defense Fund, remarked that Bayard Rustin was the only one who could pull it off.

The Fellowship of Reconciliation, CORE, and SNCC created space for the more moderate Southern Christian Leadership Conference (SCLC) to provide more moderate black leaders and the Black Church with a platform from which to change minds and affect legislation. The SCLC gave mainline white churches a platform from which to soften their attitudes, beliefs, and practices regarding race.

The Black Lives Matter movement is rising up to invigorate mainline churches, which have, in great measure, rested on the laurels of the 1960s. The pink pussy–hat dynamic of the women's marches from 2016 on sensitized ears to the cries of the #MeToo movement and emboldened the transgendering and non–binary gender communities to address the pain caused by being over-looked.

## Holding onto Lamentational Passion

I offer three theological images and one pastoral angle for the purpose of keeping the mainline churches infected with lamentational passion. I trust that if we more fully embrace these images, we may enter justice marathons at an earlier mile marker.

### *God Is Deeply Relational*

The Trinity undermines images of an autonomous, distant, self-sufficient God. Catholic feminist theologian Catherine LaCugna writes:

> Choreography suggests the partnership of movement, symmetrical but not redundant, as each dancer expresses and at the same time fulfills him/herself towards the other. In interaction and inter-course, the dancers (and the observers) experience one fluid motion of encircling, encompassing, permeating, enveloping, outstretching. There are neither leaders nor followers in the divine dance, only an eternal movement of reciprocal giving and receiving, giving again and receiving again. To shift metaphors for a moment, God is eternally begetting and being begotten, spirating and being

spirated. The divine dance is fully personal and interpersonal, expressing the essence and unity of God. The unity of the dance forbids us to think of God as solitary.[25]

## The Self Is Relational

The trinitarian God is an icon for the self-in-relation. LaCugna writes that the "substance of God exists always concretely, existentially, in persons."[26] Each person of the Trinity is interdependent, mutual, and reciprocal, not solitary or bounded. Likewise, persons do not act independently but together make up the event of personhood.

Embrace of the relational self is strengthened in times of heightened ruin and despair. In 1918, at the end of World War I, Roman Catholic theologian Hans Urs von Balthasar cited a surprising discovery: four scholars, working independently of one another, had published the same conclusion about the dialogical principle of reality. Martin Buber, Gabriel Marcel, Franz Rosenzweig (an associate of Buber), and Ferdinand Ebner had each argued that the person is not isolated but a self-in-relation.[27]

One hundred years later, America's decades-long, post-1960s devotion to the autonomy of self and nation has infiltrated and conquered the executive, congressional, and judicial branches of government. The middle class continues to dissolve, and the distance between rich and poor increases. In response, a more public and lived theology is starting to herald a more radical ecclesia of relation. Those affronted and violated by the ruling party's economic,

---

[25] Catherine Mowry LaCugna, *God for Us: The Trinity and Christian Life* (New York: Harper Collins, 1991), 272.

[26] Ibid., 245–46.

[27] Hans Urs von Balthasar, *Theo-Drama: Theological Dramatic Theory 1: Prolegomena*, trans. Graham Harrison (San Francisco: Ignatius, 1986), 626, in Brueggemann, "The Friday Voice of Faith," 16.

ethnic, racial, gender, sexual, and nationalistic violence are rising up and making noise for a more relationally just America.

## The Church Is Relational

When and where the trinitarian dance—selves turning to one another in mutual, interdependent, reciprocal relation—is performed across the landscape of history, there is ecclesia, church.

The institutional church, in my case the Anglican communion, hosts the trinitarian dance on a sacramental stage. The sacrament of baptism anoints ecclesial people:

> The ecclesial *hypostasis* [person] is created at baptism. Baptism brings about a "new reality." . . . The change is indeed ontological, not in the sense that one kind of being becomes another kind of being (watermelon becomes harp), but the new being produced by baptism is a new *person,* a new being-in-relation, a new capacity for self-transcendence, a new capacity for erotic self-expression, a new capacity for communion, a genuine instance of freedom.
>
> Those who identify with Jesus in baptism are given a new way of being in the world, now as fully personal. Putting on Christ in baptism becomes the authentic basis for a true communion among persons. . . . Baptism thus transforms solitariness and separateness into communion.[28]

## The Church Exists in the Meantime

We live in the wilderness between Egypt and Canaan. The grace of the meantime is that we are invited to pray our fallibility. We may offer to God a journey characterized by an inch forward, two

---

[28] LaCugna, *God for Us,* 263.

inches back, three inches forward. We limp along with great aspirations of taking part in the trinitarian dance, yet we fail to participate fully in it. We are tempted to relax the vise, to find thin solace in stolid skepticism and unquestioning assurance. We are tempted to sit out the dance. Naming our condition and having it blessed and anointed help us carry on.

Martin Luther understood the church as a community making its way from slavery to freedom, existing between captivity and emancipation, comprising pilgrims who are *simul justus et peccator* (at one and the same time saints and sinners). I do not mean *saint* and *sinner* as the moral and immoral characters of individual persons. Rather, these terms are emblematic of relational conditions of being connected and disconnected, inherited and dis-inherited, in communion with and estranged from community.

The space between relation and isolation is our home, from which we do not escape, and yet, which we do here and there transcend. For Luther, outbreaks of the true church are transcendence of the meantime, within but not apart from the historical church. Our confession is that the true church and the historical church are inextricably bound as one. The true church acts as an underwater spring that refreshes the often murky and stagnant waters of the historical church.

In the next chapter we go to the heart of our salvation history: the cross.

# 3

# Christ Is Love, Love Is Christ

## *Lament's Theological Home*

> *If the concept of God has any validity or any use,*
> *it can only be to make us larger, freer, and more*
> *loving. If God cannot do this, then it is time we*
> *got rid of him.*
>
> —JAMES BALDWIN, THE FIRE NEXT TIME

I met Betty in Springfield, Massachusetts, in the fall of 1987. I was part of a clinical faculty that traveled to second-tier cities to teach healthcare providers to care for people dying from AIDS—Cincinnati, Omaha, and Charlotte, to name a few. Our team led workshops for a couple of days, and then an inspirational speaker offered a final plenary keynote address to send participants home with a sense of solidarity and hope.

Betty was the speaker for the Springfield audience. Her son, Tim, had died from AIDS the previous year. Up until the final few weeks of Tim's life, Betty tightly held onto her more conservative, evangelical faith. Betty trusted that God's love was manifest through God's sacrifice of his Son for her sins. Betty believed that Jesus's sacrificial death on the cross was the only way to eternal life. Betty adored Tim *in spite of* his sexual orientation. She did not torment him with God's plan of salvation, but she did pray that he would turn to Jesus before he died. Betty wanted Tim to be saved.

Betty traveled from Kansas to Los Angeles to be with Tim during the end stage of his disease. She became part of Tim's constructed family. Over the next several weeks Betty broke daily bread with society's marginalized and erased. Each day Betty, Tim, his lover, friends, and a hospice team composed of a home health aide, nurse, social worker, and chaplain co-created comfort, peace, and right relation.

This "beloved community" began to dissolve what for Betty had been a godly command to love the sinner and hate the sin. Moreover, her fear that Tim's sexual orientation was of consequence in regard to his salvation moved from the middle to the margin of her faith.

Betty had reoriented her relation to the cross. The cross became less a plan of God and more a lived experience of Tim's constructed family, those crucified by religion, culture, and an alien disease, who lived and died for and with one another. Salvation and a sacrificial community that incites an emancipatory joy just short of heaven became one and the same. Short of heaven was enough for now.

Betty's emerging faith in a new and different way of the cross was sealed the day of Tim's death. The day before his birthday, Tim was rushed to the hospital with what was to be a fatal bout of pneumonia. After an hour or so in the emergency room, Tim was transferred to the AIDS floor. Betty sat vigil with her new family through the night and into the next day. Late in the afternoon, Betty took a breather for an hour or so. When Betty returned to the AIDS floor, she heard music, cheerful voices, and laughter. Tim's lover and friends, the nursing staff, other AIDS patients and their loved ones were throwing a birthday party for Tim, even though he was now comatose.

The cross Betty carried from the hospital was more relational, less formulaic. Hence, a sadder cross. Sad is good. Sad connects one's tears to another's and evokes comfort and joy when and where it is not expected. Sad is Tim's constructed family's invocation and benediction. Betty's cross was simpler, too, one that did not require Tim to receive a last measure of ritualized healing from a priest or pastor in order to make a way toward rest and peace. Tim's final anointing was the *deep middle* of his dying, the relational *now* into which Betty was immersed. The *deep middle* of Tim's dying mirrors Calvary:

> When Jesus saw his mother and the disciple whom he loved standing beside her, he said to his mother, "Woman, here is your son." Then he said to the disciple, "Here is your mother." And from that hour the disciple took her into his own home. (Jn 19:26–28)

Lament is a way of the cross. Lament is a foundational expression of life in Christ, the crucified for the crucified. In this chapter we explore a lived theology of lament.

## Lament's Cross Creates Life Where There Is Death, Not Death Where There Is Life

Womanist theologian Delores S. Williams reminds us that there is more to the story of the exodus than the Hebrews' release from bondage in Egypt. She inspires us to remember what we too easily forget—that the exodus was a series of events that culminated in a God-sanctioned genocide of the Canaanites and the taking of their lands.[1] The exodus of the Hebrews from Egypt to Canaan is a story of God parsing humankind into those who have been

---

[1] Delores S. Williams, *Sisters in the Wilderness: The Challenge of Womanist God-Talk* (Maryknoll, NY: Orbis Books, 1993, 2013), 133.

chosen and those who have not.[2] As such, it is a story of hope and horror. Exodus encompasses the emancipatory fire that is the cross of Tim's constructed family and Betty's pre–Los Angeles allegiance to a cross that grants life through death. By naming the terror by which the promised land was forged, we remember

> how humans have tried throughout history to destroy visions of righting relationship that involve transformation of tradition and transformation of social relations and arrangements sanctioned by the status quo. . . . Humankind is, then, redeemed through Jesus' ministerial vision of life and not through death.[3]

Lament suspends devotion to a cross that constructs Jesus as surrogate. The half-life of the satisfaction theory of the atonement is particularly short among the suffering. M. Shawn Copeland writes:

> If we follow Christ crucified with attention, reverence, and devotion, we would recognize that the tears and blood and moans of the innocent have been absorbed into our streams and rivers and swamps and seas and oceans, into the earth in which we plant and from which we harvest and eat.
>
> If we follow with attention, reverence, and devotion the moans and tears of the brutalized and burned, raped, and mutilated, enslaved and captive across the centuries, we are led to the ground beneath the cross of the crucified Jewish Jesus of Nazareth.[4]

---

[2] For a thorough historical-theological analysis of the relation of the exodus story and the cross of Jesus to American exceptionalism, see Kelly Brown Douglas, *Stand Your Ground: Black Bodies and the Justice of God* (Maryknoll, NY: Orbis Books, 2015).

[3] Williams, *Sisters in the Wilderness*, 148.

[4] M. Shawn Copeland, *Knowing Christ Crucified: The Witness of African American Religious Experience* (Maryknoll, NY: Orbis Books, 2018), 134–35.

## Lament's Cross Subdues Despair and Unleashes Joy

Tim's radically convivial dying domesticated anguish. Betty left Los Angeles with a luminosity that lifted the hearts of healthcare workers in Springfield, who would return home to more hurt than they could heal. Civil rights leader Andrew Young remembered the time Fannie Lou Hamer emerged from a week in jail with a glow around her.[5] He said that her luminous spirit brought home to him the redemptive power of imprisoned lamenters. Fannie Lou Hamer, and so many like her, knew how to lift up those who bore more pain than they thought they could bear. Historian Nishani Frazier says:

> I always think of Fannie Lou Hamer. I mean, Fannie Lou Hamer was forty-five years old, working as a sharecropper out of Mississippi. The woman had—I don't even think she had gotten past maybe sixth grade, maybe eighth grade tops—so certainly she was not the most literate person. And the woman could move people. I mean, I think her story is a story that you tell above anyone else's. Because it literally speaks to the sense of the nobody being able to move everybody. And the impact is just powerful. I mean, you know, it's almost like—why couldn't Dr. King move somebody? He graduated from Morehouse College, he had a doctorate— I mean, my God, if he didn't, he'd just be lazy. And here's Fannie Lou Hamer, and she is *dy-na-mic*. And the woman is close to being illiterate. So when you tell that story, I think that changes things.[6]

---

[5] Andrew Young, "Minister of the Beloved Community," lecture, Iliff School of Theology, Denver, Colorado, 2000.

[6] William Blaine-Wallace, "A Pastoral Psychology of Lament: Pastoral Method, Priestly Act, Prophetic Witness," PhD diss., Catholic University of Brabant (Tilburg, the Netherlands, 2009), 160.

Friends of Mrs. Hamer talk about how she pushed fear aside. When fellow protesters were scared, she did not talk them down. She started humming or singing a spiritual. Soon the crowd joined in.

Bernice Johnson Reagon, founder of the musical group Sweet Honey in the Rock, bears witness to the same power of lamentational relation. While a student at Albany State College, Reagon was jailed for leading a protest march. Reflecting on her experience in a makeshift jail crammed with sister lamenters, Bernice said: "In jail my voice changed, my voice deepened." Jail was Reagon's Juilliard.[7]

On November 15, 2015, a twenty-four-year-old African American male, Jamar Clark, was shot and killed by two Minneapolis police officers.[8] After his funeral the funeral procession drove by the police station to show support for protesters who had occupied the site for several days. Barbara A. Holmes, then the new president of United Theological Seminary of the Twin Cities, and a part of the funeral procession, writes:

> The funeral procession entered the tight pathway surrounded by Black Lives Matter activists and allies. Every few feet, a door of a funeral car would be flung open and the occupants would jump out and dance as if their lives depended on the movement. The hip-hop music blasted from the cars; the respect being paid was primal and authentic. They were performing authenticity and grief so profound that only feet could speak. Our hearts were breaking, our feet were moving, and there was joy unspeakable and full of glory.[9]

---

[7] Bernice Johnson Reagon, "Singing Warrior," lecture, Ilif School of Theology, Denver, Colorado, 2000.

[8] Editorial Board, "Jamar Clark Protest Ended Well Despite Miscues by City Police," *Star Tribune* (March 22, 2017).

[9] Barbara A. Holmes, *Joy Unspeakable: Contemplative Practices of the Black Church* (Minneapolis: Fortress Press, 2017), 160.

The solidarity unleashed by lament's cross was also expressed through a community desecrated by the genocide of the Tutsis by the Hutus in Rwanda in April 1994.[10] Two hundred Tutsis from several families fled to a convent, a little more than two hundred yards from the United Nations peace envoy compound, to escape the Hutus. The Hutus found, rounded up, and hacked to death children, women, and men and buried them in a large pit.

Years later the children, spouses, siblings, and friends of the executed Tutsis worked with nuns behind the convent to exhume loved ones. They identified them, as best as they could, mostly from fabric remnants. They washed and placed the bones in separate piles: skulls with skulls, thigh bone with thigh bone. They reconfigured bodies and placed them in coffins draped in white and marked with a purple cross. While they worked, they sang, prayed, laughed, and cried. In the evenings they shared memories and participated in conversations about embracing the future, learning reconciliation, and practicing forgiveness. They understood these conversations to be as much a part of the burial rite as the final burial service. After the burial they kept the conversations alive so that the ghosts of their dead would rest and remain in peace.[11]

## Lament's Cross Reconciles

Public lament creates a stronger possibility for reconciliation between perpetrators of violence, tyranny, and power abuses, and their victims.[12] Reconciliation begins with the victims' public

---

[10] Gilbert Ndahayo, producer, director, writer, *Behind the Convent*, motion picture (Rwanda: Ndahayo Productions, 2008).

[11] The original account of this story appears in Blaine-Wallace, "A Pastoral Psychology of Lament," 39.

[12] My construction of lament as reconciliation originated in William Blaine-Wallace, "Lamentation as Justice-Making," in *Injustice and the Care of Souls: Taking Oppression Seriously in Pastoral Care*, ed. Sheryl A. Kujawa-Holbrook and Karen B. Montagno (Minneapolis: Fortress Press, 2009), 188–90.

testimony—if at all possible in the presence of their perpetrators. A good percentage of processes of reconciliation fail because the victims are decentered. Extraneous recipes for reconciliation are imposed on victims by those who presume to act on their behalf. The voices of the victims are patronized or, at worst, silenced. When the voices of victims are at the center of the reconciliation process, ground is broken for forgiveness and healing.

Archbishop Desmond Tutu, after the first public hearings of the Truth and Reconciliation Commission in South Africa, received a letter from a radio listener who heard the broadcast testimonies of several victims and was moved to write and share this poem:

> The world is wept.
> Blood and pain seep into our listening; into our
>     wounded souls.
> The sound of your sobbing is my own weeping;
> Your wet handkerchief my pillow for a past so
>     exhausted it cannot rest—not yet.
> Speak, weep, look, listen for us all.
> Oh, people of the silent hidden past,
> let your stories scatter seeds into our lonely
>     frightened winds.
> Sow more, until the stillness of this land can
>     soften, can dare to hope and smile and sing;
> Until the ghosts can dance unshackled, until our
>     lives can know your sorrows
> And be healed.[13]

Public lament also creates a stronger possibility for reconciliation between nations in conflict. Conflict resolution expert Olga Botcharova writes that violated nations move to knee-jerk positions

---

[13] Desmond Tutu, *No Future without Forgiveness* (New York: Random House, 1999), 119.

of invincibility that exacerbate further violence because they do not take the necessary time to grieve losses and attend to suffering.[14] Botcharova found that an intentional, timely, and persistent sharing of the pain caused by violation opens space for options other than retaliation.

The mistakes and missed opportunities regarding our national response to 9/11 continue to haunt us. What if America had been encouraged to grieve for more than the ten days of flamboyant mourning prescribed and abruptly terminated by President Bush, who called for "an end to grief"?[15] Possibly we would be less complacent about our hasty responses to global threats that continue to dominate foreign policy. Attention to our suffering and sorrow for more than the gilded ten days may have yielded a heightened experience of "humility, vulnerability, impressionability, and dependence,"[16] which might then have moved us beyond the position "of the paranoid victim who regenerates infinitely the justifications for war."[17]

Judith Butler calls our post-9/11 behavior a disease born of the neglect of claiming and lamenting our vulnerability:

A narrative form emerges to compensate for the enormous narcissistic wound opened up by the public display of our physical vulnerability. Our response, accordingly, is not to enter into international coalitions where we understand ourselves to be working with institutionally established routes to consensus building. We relegate the United Nations to a second-order deliberative body, and insist instead

---

[14] Olga Botcharova, "Implementation of Track Two Diplomacy," in *Forgiveness and Reconciliation: Religion, Public Policy and Conflict Transformation*, ed. S. J. Helmick and R. L. Petersen (Radnor, PA: Templeton Foundation Press, 2001), 279–304.

[15] Judith Butler, *Precarious Life: The Powers of Mourning and Violence* (London: Verso, 2004), 149.

[16] Ibid., 150.

[17] Ibid.

on American unilateralism. And subsequently we ask, who is with us? Who is against us? As a result, we respond to the exposure to vulnerability with an assertion of US "leadership," showing once again the contempt we have for international coalitions that are not built and led by us.[18]

### Lament's Cross Is the Antidote to Congregational Somnolence

Mainline churches[19] of North America, on the whole, do not privilege cruciform relations that renew community; they do not radiate joy that transcends despair; and they do not reconcile those who are estranged. Carlyle Marney, iconic pastor of Myers Park Baptist Church in Charlotte, North Carolina, during the 1960s, said in regard to matters of justice, particularly race matters, that "the churches of Charlotte, one of the most religious cities in America, don't have enough gas to get from here to Wadesboro."[20] That's about fifty miles.

Several years ago I interviewed Ruby Sales about mainline churches' lethargy. The interview took place at Bates College during the Martin Luther King Jr. Day events. Sales was on campus to deliver the sermon at the Sunday night MLK worship service.

Sales, founder and current director of Spirit House in Washington, DC, is an honored veteran of the civil rights movement. She was a member of the Student Nonviolent Coordinating Commit-

---

[18] Ibid., 7.

[19] As noted in Chapter 2, by "mainline churches" I mean Protestant churches, the majority of Christians in North America. By "Protestant," I mean the Baptist, Episcopal, Lutheran, Methodist, Presbyterian, and United Church of Christ denominations. I imagine Roman Catholic parishes in many ways mirror the spirit of Protestant congregations. I do not know enough about Roman Catholic parishes to make more definitive claims about them.

[20] John Carey, *A Pilgrim's Progress* (Macon, GA: Mercer University Press, 1981), 45.

tee (SNCC) as a teenager. In August 1965, Sales and fellow SNCC members were working in Lowndes County, Alabama, to integrate public places and to register black voters after the passage several days before of the Voting Rights Act. Sales and three other SNCC workers—seminarian Jonathan Daniels, Father Richard Morrisroe, and activist Joyce Bailey—went to a general store in Haynesville for sodas shortly after being released from jail. The man behind the cash register was Tom Coleman, a construction worker and unpaid special deputy sheriff. Sales was the first to pay. Daniels was behind her. Angry that Sales, a black woman, was standing in front of a white man, Coleman pulled a shotgun from under the counter and aimed it at seventeen-year-old Sales. Daniels pushed Sales aside just as Coleman fired. Daniels was martyred, and Father Morrisroe was seriously injured.

The following is my condensed interview of Ruby Sales, one of two, the Sunday afternoon before the MLK service at Bates College:

*Bill:* Do you think mainline church is capable of jubilation?

*Ruby:* No, because in a socially constructed world, whiteness is predicated on power and things. That's not something to shout about in church. [The mainline churches] need to reconstruct themselves.

*Bill:* So, how do we reconstruct the church?

*Ruby:* By having religion not undergird white supremacy and power. Have it undergird human freedom. It would be a testifying church [based on] thanksgiving, realizing that it is a gift to wake up in the morning. Do you remember when the Kenyan guy came to Episcopal Divinity School? I'll never forget. We were in worship, and he was leading the service that day.

*Bill:* No, I was not in worship that morning.

*Ruby:* Oh, God, you were not there. He came out in this long African robe, and he said, "Let's *celebrate.* I want to thank God for this *morning.*" People looked at him like he was barbaric.

*Bill:* Why did they look at him that way?

*Ruby:* Because he was experiencing God in a different way. Because he was starting with thanksgiving. Because he wanted to praise God . . . for the journey. As difficult as his life had been, he thought that there had been milestones along the way that were worth celebrating. And they didn't get that. He stopped in the middle of the service and said, "Well, I must be doing something wrong."

*Bill:* I'm just not sure mainline church can get to that place.

*Ruby:* Bill, you got to look at your *history*. History becomes the cornerstone for how we understand and act out a meaning of God. So, if you come from a history of enslavement, industrialism, I mean, and all of the other "isms" . . .

*Bill:* So we have to shout about our bondage to materialism?

*Ruby:* I once was lost, but now I'm found; was blind but now I see.

*Bill:* And we are lost in our affluence?

*Ruby:* Numbed in your affluence. Because in effect, you can't pray. . . . You can't shout when you're *numb*. And see, part of being white—

*Bill:* See, that's why I think we're walking around inarticulately wailing. I mean in depression, in numbness, in road rage, in boredom . . . and how do we find, how do we come together in our enslavement? How do we come together and shout through our enslavement?

*Ruby:* This is how. I say, you know, black people are not the only people who suffer from tremendous loss. To be white is to lose your connections with your ancestors, to lose your historical experiences. You kill the connection to your past. I talk about whiteness—not as a privilege, but as a death. You kill your connection to the fact that your grandmother was an Irish peasant. You forget to remember that in England your great-great-grandmother stood on the corner begging for food.

Mainline religion in America is immunized against lament's cross by a grand narrative of whiteness as material sufficiency and self-actualization. Devotion to sufficiency clouds memory and stifles the desire to discover our past. This immunization has made us anemic. Mainline parishes do not provide enough space for parishioners to listen respectfully, attentively, and curiously to one another regarding ancient histories of hurt and hardship. We have drifted off the moorings of the troubles seen by our elders and ancestors. We have washed up on the more barren shores of the successes we've achieved. Our challenge is to "re-member" the ligaments that attach us to neighbors near and far, that strengthen us for greater and more consequential relations with a world groaning in distress and grappling for liberation. The more we know and pray the legacies of our suffering, sorrows, and trauma, the more distance we will have closed, the more difference we will have erased, between Darfur and New England.

What if mainline congregations engaged in inquiry? What if relational space was made for parishioners to learn about and share one another's family histories? I trust the research would render more nuanced, impassioned, vulnerable, and engaged conversations. I trust the conversations would vivify our lives together. I trust that a more honest sense of our journeys may become a thorn in the side of our theologies of glory.

What we forget about our own histories affects the claims and commitments we make about our particular faith. When we embrace our cruciform histories, what German Catholic theologian Johann Baptist Metz calls "dangerous memory," we are stirred to loosen the grip of our more arrogant claims about God and the church:

Memory has a fundamental theological importance as what may be termed . . . solidarity in memory with the dead and the conquered which breaks the grip of history as a history of triumph and conquest interpreted dialectically or as evolution.[21]

The following is from my second interview with Ruby Sales, the morning after the MLK worship service:

*Bill:* Ruby, building on what you said last night—it meant so much to me—that Dr. King was the beneficiary of a long fermenting movement. He walked in front of people like your mom and your dad.
*Ruby:* No, he walked behind.
*Bill:* He walked behind?
*Ruby:* He walked behind people like my mother, my father, my grandmother, his mother, his father, the people in the church that he talks about, the old women in the church that he grew up with, who claimed him very early as their own precious little Martin, and so he walked behind, we walked behind that generation . . . who really held the community open for us.
*Bill:* The movement was carved from the heart of the elderly women in church?
*Ruby:* I would say it was carved out of the hearts and hands . . . hearts *and* hands, and work, hard work of the women, of black women in the church. They were the carriers of the dream. They were the ones who gave you two dollars in a handkerchief when you went away to college. They were the ones who had the oratorical contests. They were the ones who had interpretive dance contests. They were the ones who fertilized your intellect and your creativity, and who made you believe that you could be somebody in a world that said that you didn't exist. *That* was not a word in

---

[21] Johann Baptist Metz, *Faith in History and Society: Toward a Practical Fundamental Theology* (New York: Seabury Press, 1980), 184.

their vocabulary, that you didn't exist. So they were pumping us up for excellence . . . in a world that said that we were inferior. There was nothing in my vocabulary that said inferior, *nothing*. Because these *extra*ordinary women made me feel that I was a special child—as Alice Walker talks about, in terms of "womanist"—I mean if you're one of these special black girls who talk back to the world, who's sassy, who's precocious instead of being beaten down—you're egged on. And so I was one of those little black girls who was egged on.

*Bill:* Where did these women find and nurture their passion?

*Ruby:* They found and nurtured their passion in their relationship with God. They were visionaries. They had the capacity to work not only for what was there today, but what could be possible tomorrow. They were the ones who could see down the road. They were the ones who understood—with a very deep, deep understanding—that injustice didn't last forever. And that you had to prepare people to be able to work for that day when it didn't exist, and to work to bring it about.

I am sixty-eight years old. I still warm to the words "you are a special child." I still want two dollars put in my backpack on my way out the door to a retreat. In many ways I was carved by the heart and hands of my grandmother Lillie, a long-time, devout member of Cobb Memorial Baptist Church in East Rockingham, North Carolina, located near what was once the Saffe Mill Village, where she worked hard and long. Lillie was "church" for me. I need the wise, tested, sculpting love that elders in the church have to offer.

Mainline parishes, more and more, objectify the elders as the "graying church, the dying church." We walk in front and away from them in search of "younger families, seekers, and millennials." We patronize the elders. We are apt to silence their voice and neglect their wisdom.

## Church at the Foot of Lament's Cross

Mainline churches have too little money. Preoccupation with material sustainability leaves little energy and less focus for embodying lament's cross with the elders and others. Mainline churches have too much money. Our quest for upward mobility keeps us on the go, with little time to slow down for a steadying presence at the foot of lament's cross. As a result, loneliness and anxiety manifest in subtle ways that infect our life together. The hunger for an ecclesial design that mirrors Tim's constructed family is unnamed and therefore difficult to address. The mainline churches have a low-grade fever that leaves us lethargic, ornery, and, as Ruby Sales suggests, numb. Sadly, the cure, lamentational relation, readily available, escapes us. On the other hand, faith communities that more regularly embrace lament's cross often do not score well when measured by mainline churches' culturally imposed indicators of survival and success: healthy budgets, buildings that do not leak and crack, pews that are full. There does not seem to be much hope for the future of the churches in North America.

There is hope, however—a different kind of hope that mainline churches have more or less abandoned. Our future hope is our past history. Imagine post-Christian house churches that mirror the pre-Christian house churches that witnessed Jesus's execution—his mother, the beloved disciple, an aunt, and a cherished friend. Tim's constructed family. From these more organic, dependent, fragile Christian communities emerges a renewed ecclesiology that sustains relations that survive time. House churches also transcend ever-dissolving denominational demarcations.

Most important, we do not need to start over. Starting over is too daunting to imagine. Church at the foot of lament's cross, as Luther's theology of the true and historical church suggests, need not exist in opposition to the mainline churches. The cruciform church can infuse and, over time, help revive an infirm institution.

A cruciform church can revive a solvency-minded institution that presently seems to get about eleven miles to the gallon on the open road, eight miles in the city. Our challenge is to shift our priority to a different kind of sustainability. We need to muster up enough courage to trust the kind of relation that is at the heart of salvation history.

Age-old choruses of lament-filled hallelujahs ring through our history. Hallelujahs begin with Genesis 1:1–2, when the Spirit moved over chaos and emptiness, and they resound through time. Sunday in the narthex, after Eucharist, a couple who lost a child years before to a car accident embraces a couple who just lost a child to a drug overdose. Other parishioners gather around to pile on love. Each day Amens! such as these re-point the crumbling mortar between a few more bricks on the tired facade of Christendom. When and as we privilege these Amens! in the daily life of our Christian communities, the reformation of our tradition progresses. "God is the 'beyond' in the midst of life," as Bonhoeffer reminds us.[22]

In the next chapter we reflect on the one Jesus summoned from the cross.

---

[22] Dietrich Bonhoeffer, in Martin E. Marty, *Dietrich Bonhoeffer's Letters and Papers from Prison* (Princeton, NJ: Princeton University Press, 2011), 112.

4

# God off the Rails

## Lament and the Suffering God

*Nobody knows de trouble I've seen*
*Nobody knows de trouble but Jesus*
*Nobody knows de trouble I've seen*
*Glory Hallelujah!*

—NEGRO SPIRITUAL

### God Beholds

*"You are the God who sees me."*
—GENESIS 16:13A, NIV

Recently, I received a call from a person I meet with for counseling. Jason was concerned, again, about his teenaged daughter, Carolyn. The concern didn't warrant a trip to the emergency room or a call to 911 or Maine's mental health crisis line, resources that are listed on my after-hours practice line. However, waiting until our next meeting would not suffice. I understood Jason's need to talk. The meantime is most of the time.

When our children are in trouble, or when we perceive that their life situation might create greater struggle or increase hardship, we are moved. My daughter, Sarah Frances, called a few days ago and shared news that she and her husband, Owen, were expecting. Jubilation! A second child! After the call, during the night, I awoke to anxious thoughts. How can they afford two children in daycare? Probably 25 percent of their income. Would it be possible for either Owen or Sarah Frances to be a stay-at-home parent? Yet if a friend had called and shared news of a child's pregnancy and concern about the financial ramifications, my response would have been more philosophical and contained.

The love of a child is proximate—near and immediate. It is also determinative. We are affected by and act in relation to the child's particular situation in regard to the moment at hand. Moreover, we craft and modulate the love to match what might be best for the child. What is the most effective content, shape, and timing of my regard? What shall I say and not say, do and not do? With whom do I confer about my possible intervention? A delicate dance.

Emmanuel Levinas constructs the character of paternal love into an ethic of love for neighbor: "I think that *the Human* consists precisely in opening oneself to the death of the other, to being preoccupied with his or her death."[1] In other words, what goes for Sarah Frances and Owen applies to Jason and Carolyn as well, not to mention the majority of children on free breakfast and lunch programs in the public schools of central Maine. Unreserved love unnerves. Simone Weil writes, "Human existence is so fragile a thing and exposed to such dangers that I cannot love without trembling."[2] Levinas's ethic is high moral ground.

---

[1] Emmanuel Levinas, *Alterity and Transcendence* (New York: Columbia University Press, 1999), 157–58.

[2] Simone Weil, *Gravity and Grace* (New York: Routledge, 2002; originally published 1952), xiii.

Most often, as Mark Freeman writes in *Priority of the Other,* we *look* at rather than *see* our neighbor.[3] Looking at the other privileges the "eye" of the dominant looker, the observing self, and objectifies the one who is looked at. How many parents of the children in the area schools are victims of Big Pharma's seeding of the opioid crisis? While my question conveys concern, the concern is sculpted from my particular, more progressive Christian lens. *Looking* is resonant with Martin Buber's *I-It* relation. *Seeing* the other suggests a diminishment of self, a shift from self to self-in-relation, mutuality *between* neighbors, Buber's *I-Thou* relation. How many of the children's parents have I broken bread with? Levinas's ethic of responsibility *for* the neighbor arguably is more radical than mutuality *between* neighbors, and therefore beyond self-in-relation. It is Buber to the next power. It is relation outside self, *ex-centric.*[4] Freeman writes that "by 'living ex-centrically,' I am referring to living in a way that is more oriented toward those objects and activities that work centrifugally, to move us beyond the centripetal pull of the ego."[5]

Catastrophic occurrences like the mass shooting at Sandy Hook Elementary School in 2012 transport us to "ex-centric" relation. We cling to community. But what about life on an ordinary Thursday morning, like this morning, when my present concern is whether to have our driveway sanded today or wait until after tomorrow's freezing rain? The ex-centric question today, having recently met with the mother of a child who is on the verge of expulsion from school, is this: When and how might I become a Big Brother volunteer and befriend a thirteen-year-old whose anger-management problem most likely is related to his father abandoning him? That

---

[3] Mark Freeman, *The Priority of the Other: Thinking and Living beyond the Self* (New York: Oxford University Press, 2014), 108.

[4] Ibid., 30.

[5] Ibid., 182.

this adolescent would occupy my Wednesday evening or Saturday morning is, in the language of Levinas, the fulfillment of the sixth commandment, Thou Shall Not Kill.[6] Neighbor is beheld, before whom we are relationally bowed in a particularly consequential way.

The love of one's children, universalized in Levinas's ethic of the other, is a glimpse of the Father's love for the Son, the Father whom Jesus addresses from the cross, the Father whom we address from places of our desolations and diminishments.

Delores S. Williams reflects on the Father's love with respect to Hagar, twice in the wilderness: once pregnant with child (Gn 16:1–15) and next accompanied by child (Gn 21:14–21); once fleeing from, next banished by, the detritus of Abraham and Sarah's entanglement over progeny.[7]

The issue at hand during Hagar's first flight to the desert was not the evil of slavery. The immediate issue was pregnant Hagar, alone in and at the mercy of the wilderness: "The angel of the LORD said to her, 'Return to your mistress, and submit to her'" (Gn 16:9). Bad theology, good advice. Hagar responds: "She gave this name to the LORD who spoke to her: 'You are the God who sees me,' for she said, 'I have now seen the One who sees me'" (Gn 16:13, NIV). The name of the God to whom Hagar ascribes sight is *El ro'i*, "God Who sees me,"[8] a name different from the name of a God of patriarchy, the God of her oppressors.[9] Good theology.

---

[6] Emmanuel Levinas, *Ethics and Infinity* (Pittsburgh: Duquesne University Press, 1995), 89.

[7] Delores S. Williams, *Sisters in the Wilderness: The Challenge of Womanist God-Talk* (Maryknoll, NY: Orbis Books, 1993, 2013), 15–31.

[8] Translation by Robert Alter, *The Hebrew Bible: A Translation with Commentary* (New York: W. W. Norton, Company, 2018).

[9] Helmer Ringgren, *Israelite Religion*, trans. David E. Green (Philadelphia: Fortress Press, 1966), 21–22, cited in Williams, *Sisters in the Wilderness*, 22.

## God Provides

Survival is also the issue at hand during the second trip to the wilderness, when Abraham banished Hagar and her son, Ishmael. When mother and child ran out of the water Abraham had provided for the journey, Hagar

> went off and sat down about a bowshot away, for she thought, "I cannot watch the boy die." And as she sat there, she began to sob. God heard the boy crying, and the angel of God called to Hagar from heaven and said to her, "What is the matter, Hagar? Do not be afraid; God has heard the boy crying as he lies there. Lift the boy up and take him by the hand, for I will make him into a great nation." Then God opened her eyes and she saw a well of water. So she went and filled the skin with water and gave the boy a drink. God was with the boy as he grew up. He lived in the desert and became an archer. While he was living in the Desert of Paran, his mother got a wife for him from Egypt. (Gn 21:16–21)

Williams notes that God gave Hagar the vision to see "survival resources where she saw none before."[10] Also in the spirit of survival, Hagar chooses a wife for Ishmael who is of her own Egyptian heritage, a heritage offering more agency and autonomy for women, in contrast with the more patriarchal culture of Abraham and Sarah.[11] Williams sees Hagar collaborating with God to develop strategies for surviving life in the wilderness, life between bondage and freedom. Williams associates their collaboration with the survival/quality-of-life needs of African American women and their children:

---

[10] Williams, *Sisters in the Wilderness,* 30.
[11] Ibid.

This Hagar symbolism affirms such qualities as defiance; risk-taking; independence; endurance when endurance gives no promise; the stamina to hold things together for the family (even without the help of a mate); the ability in poverty to make a way out of no way; the courage to initiate political action in the public arena; and a close personal relation with God.[12]

Williams's association serves as a critique of liberation theologies that do not adequately address how nomads and pilgrims are and are not faring in the wilderness, a territory oriented to survival for those who move around for sustenance and those who move forward for freedom. Liberation theologies, infused with a passion oriented to a freer future, arguably pay less attention to the present, the place where matters of provision take precedent.

The love of God beholds us in the immediacy of our lives and relations at the same time as God walks with us toward a new day. The particularities of our lives and relations in the present affect and shape the character of God's love for us. That God *sees* us in the *meantime*—the wilderness between bondage and freedom—forms the way we lament from one moment to the next.

We may and often do lament the bigger matters. We decry racism in the United States. We out Big Pharma, naming Big Pharma's role in the opioid crisis. We scream about the withdrawal of the United States from the Paris climate agreement. We raise our fists for "Medicare for All." As these lofty laments take precedence, we are more apt to wear down and lose heart. The arcs of big laments are long, little progress is seen, and breakthroughs are too rare. How much MSNBC can we take? An ecclesiology of lament invites us to pare down large laments to a size we can manage in order that they may incite greater agency for action *now*, in the wilderness

---

[12] Ibid., 108.

between bondage and freedom. Prayerful conversation about how we and our relations are *affected* by big laments thickens community, vivifies solidarity, and inspires commitment.

I know of a local parish that makes space to lament regularly and communally the effects of big laments brought near. Theresa continues to share what mothering is like in the context of an adult son addicted to heroin and methadone—fist fights in the street, a stolen car, prison, and rejection by family. Jessica continues to wail about a very debilitating chronic disease, an experience made worse by the subtle and not so subtle ways that the local healthcare delivery system slights and demeans her because she does not get better on their watch, by their diagnoses and prescriptions, and within their time frames. Theresa's troubles and Jessica's sense of helplessness and institutional shaming are seen for a time, until next time. Hallelujah!

When parishioners are provided safer spaces to lament the local effects of addictions, global warming, race relations, and healthcare, matters are more apt to be taken to hand in a way that rises above the more benign talk and demeanor of social ministry and pastoral care committees. Pockets of lament come together to form a lament choir that impassions parishioners to engage the powers and principalities. As activist Glenda Hope declares, "No! First we grieve and then we march."[13]

## God Suffers

*Then Jesus gave a loud cry and breathed his last.*
*And the curtain of the temple was torn in two,*
*from top to bottom.*

—MARK 15:37–38

---

[13] In Sharon Thornton, *Broken Yet Beloved: A Pastoral Theology of the Cross* (St. Louis: Chalice Press, 2002), 188.

> *At that moment the curtain of the temple was torn*
> *in two, from top to bottom. The earth shook, and*
> *the rocks were split.*
>
> —MATTHEW 27:51

At the moment of Jesus's death, God came unhinged. In *Preaching Mark in Two Voices*, Gary W. Charles writes:

> The passive voice of the verb, *schizo*, indicates that this rendering is the divine response to the death of Jesus; the tense and meaning of this verb suggest a violent, completed, and decisive action. As God rends the veil *(katapetasma)* of the sanctuary *(naos)*, that which divided the holy from the profane is removed.[14]

God's wailing violently, aggressively, uncontrollably crosses the boundaries of the acceptable and sane, the predictable and containable. God is out there—out there as parents are when the incomprehensible abyss that is the death of a child severs one's self, shakes one loose from the sturdiest moorings, splits one's world wide open, leaving one wholly exposed. Catherine of Siena (1347–80) wrote that God is *pazzo d'amore* (made crazy from love).[15]

Dietrich Bonhoeffer, several months away from execution, reached out to God gone mad. Prose could not hold his offering. Poetry was the better hand:

> Men go to God when he is sore bestead,
> Find him poor and scorned, without shelter or
> bread,

---

[14] Brian K. Blount and Gary W. Charles, *Preaching Mark in Two Voices* (Louisville, KY: Westminster John Knox Press, 2005), 240.

[15] Susan Cahill, *Wise Women: 2000 Years of Spiritual Writing by Women* (New York: Norton, 1996), 74.

> Whelmed under weight of the wicked, the
> > weak,
> the dead:
> Christians stand by God in his hour of griev-
> > ing.[16]

Bonhoeffer came to believe that God "is weak and powerless in the world, and that is precisely the way, the only way, in which he is with us and helps us."[17] I imagine this confession is the answer to a prayerful desire Bonhoeffer offered years earlier in a conversation:

> I remember a conversation that I had in America thirteen years ago with a young French pastor. We were asking ourselves quite simply what we wanted to do with our lives. He said that he would like to become a saint. I think it is quite likely he became one. At the time I was very much impressed, but I disagreed with him, and said, in effect, that I should like to learn to have faith. For a long time I did not realize the depth of the contrast. I thought I could acquire faith by trying to live a holy life, or something like it. . . . I discovered later, and I'm still discovering up to this moment, that it is only by living completely in this world that one learns to have faith. One must completely abandon any attempt to make something of oneself, whether it be a saint, or a converted sinner, or a churchman (the so-called priestly type!), a righteous man or an unrighteous one, a sick man or a healthy one. By this-worldliness I mean living unreservedly in life's duties, problems, successes and failures, experiences and perplexities. In so doing we throw ourselves completely into the arms of God, taking seriously, not our own sufferings, but those of

---

[16] Dietrich Bonhoeffer, *Letters and Papers from Prison* (New York: Collier Books, 1972), 348–49.

[17] Ibid., 360.

God in the world—watching with Christ in Gethsemane.
That, I think, is faith, that is *metanoia*.[18]

Bonhoeffer's *metanoia* was more than a decade in the making,
unfolding in, under, around, and through Nazi rule. God, for Bonhoeffer, was slowly and steadily "pushed out of the world and onto
the cross."[19] Theological belief was transposed into faith as relation
with the weak at the mercy of abject and insidious evil.

My own *metanoia* from belief in a theology of the cross to faith
in a cruciform God and life was about a decade in the making. In
1985, I became director of the hospice program at Grady Hospital,
the large, public hospital mostly for Atlanta's indigent poor and
African American communities. I brought to the position several
years of participation in hospice, which, then, was mostly a white,
middle-class movement recently turned into a healthcare delivery
system by the passage of the Hospice Medicare benefit in 1983.
The initial inspiration for hospice, I believe, was in part a means of
relief for two-income families too burdened to do what families a
generation before them had done—attend to those among them
who were dying.

Once at Grady, I realized that I had little to offer in terms
of hospice experience. The families we served had an immense
amount of wisdom and knowledge about caring for their own, and
a nearer-to-the-ground faith in the God who provides. I witnessed
what Delores Williams names through her examination of the
Hagar story. Grady taught me the most and best of what I know
about the "uncanny resilience of the mothering/nurturing/caring/
enduring and resistance capacities" of those "in the wilderness of
America . . . birthing a spirit of hope" for their communities.[20]

---

18 Ibid., 369–70.
19 Ibid., 360.
20 Williams, *Sisters in the Wilderness*, 208.

Moreover, I came to spend the biggest part of my week among those who I had previously encountered only at the edges of my daily life.

Soon after I arrived at Grady, I was summoned to a patient's room. A young woman, a medical resident, was holding the hand of a young man near death, sweating and shaking, his eyes wide and registering fear. This was my first encounter with a person with AIDS. Over the next few years, Grady was inundated with mostly young, middle-class white men with AIDS, many of whom did not imagine that one day they would join the other patients at Grady, their families, communities, and healthcare providers having abandoned them. Many of those dying from AIDS in the Grady system ended up in our hospice. The African American, God-will-provide spirit that permeated our program welcomed them with wide open arms. As I mentioned in the Introduction, my years at Grady represent my strongest participation in what the civil rights movement often referred to as the "beloved community."

My experience suggests that it is unlikely that belief rises to faith without the refining fire of the sorrow, suffering, and trauma of life-the-way-it-really-is. As for the church, sound preaching, good liturgy, gritty adult education, and spiritual formation opportunities take us to the lip of the abyss but not into it. Church renewal hangs, in large measure, on our courage to name where and how we are pushed out of the world and onto the cross. Such participation cuts through the nicer and safer discourses of life together and inspires us to offer our fragile wherewithal, broken hearts, and exhausted spirits to one another. Hearty dialogue reveals the "God who hides in order not to be found where humans want to find God, finds God where God wills to be found."[21]

---

[21] Steven D. Paulson, "Luther on the Hidden God," *Word and World* 19, no. 4 (1995): 363.

## God as Suffering Other

When I am called across thresholds of relative order into the chaos of broken persons and communities, and when I try to grab hold amid the tremors and terrors of my own lived experience, I find myself steadied by the Father wrenched loose and left open by the gaping diminishment that is the loss of the Father's Son.[22] Our suffering, too, unhinges the sanity of God. Last week the veil of the temple was torn anew by the horror of the death of a friend's son from an opioid overdose. Moreover, unabridged love goes crazy at the role corporate greed played in this young man's death.

Saint Paul writes: "and if [we are] children, then [we are] heirs, heirs of God and joint heirs with Christ" (Rom 8:17a). Might this mean that God becomes the pattern for bonds between neighbors that are stronger than mutuality, bonds that undo us? My brokenness renders the neighbor mute. The broken neighbor renders me inarticulate. When neighbors are made crazy by love, their speechless bond is the beginning of new life.

Again, Kathleen M. O'Connor's *Lamentations and the Tears of the World* comes to mind. She writes passionately about the inspired restraint in Lamentations, a text in which God's utter silence speaks loudly and devotedly:

> Surprisingly, the book does express hope, but only in the unsteady, halting, and tenuous way known to survivors of cataclysm, trauma, depression, and loss. Hope appears and disappears, elusive as the future itself. If God spoke, God's words would diminish the voices of pain, wash over them,

---

[22] I first presented my reflections on God as suffering Other in William Blaine-Wallace, "A Pastoral Psychology of Lament: Pastoral Method, Priestly Act, Prophetic Witness," PhD diss., Catholic University of Brabant (Tilburg, the Netherlands, 2009), 74.

and crowd them out. Even one word from God would take up too much space.[23]

The human spirit aches for Another's inspired restraint.

When other becomes Other, conventional pastoral rhetoric borders on the blasphemous. Who would say to God, "Say more about that"? Rather, on holy ground we leave our tongues stuck to the roof of our mouth. We slow down thinner, anxious discourse to create dialogic space. In this space we are allowed, even invited, to complete sentences of deep diminishment. The babble of regret and longing, incubated in silence, loosely formed as utterances, and emancipated in the presence of respectful and curious beholders transposes wailing into lament.

More and more, space for completion of such sentences is sparse. Religion and psychotherapy are tempted to give answers and expect visitors and consumers to trim and squeeze their sentences into the discursive frames of their particular doctrines, theories, and techniques born of the *restitution narrative*, the ridiculous expectations of religion and healthcare for us to get better, be well, or else. Spaces for the completion of respectfully, curiously waited for, gingerly shaped utterances are increasingly rare in the church and therapy worlds. The fresher spaces for the transposition of wailing into lament often are outside the circles of convention and propriety.

## God and the Hospice at Mission Hill

*After Auschwitz, no theology:*
*the numbers on the forearms*

---

[23] Kathleen M. O'Connor, *Lamentations and the Tears of the World* (Maryknoll, NY: Orbis Books, 2002), 85–86.

> *of the inmates of extermination*
> *are the telephone numbers of God,*
> *numbers that do not answer*
> *and now are disconnected, one by one.*
>    —YEHUDA AMICHAI, "OPEN CLOSED OPEN"

From 1989 to 1993, I served as executive director of a regional hospice in greater Boston, which opened an inpatient AIDS hospice, the Hospice at Mission Hill.[24] At the hospice the matter of God was large because God mattered so much. The religious languages brought into the midst of the hospice community by residents from diverse religious backgrounds were no longer in storage. Suffering has us dust off and vivify the matter of God. Residents discovered that the religious buckets brought across the threshold of the hospice were too small for the spirit of relation encountered there. Because God mattered at the place of their dying, bigger buckets were quickly fashioned. Big enough buckets caught the spirituality of relation.

In Yehuda Amichai's poignant poem above, the God the residents phoned here and there over the course of their lives, and much more often over the course of their dying, did not answer. Still, the nature of relations among those living and dying at the hospice were witnessed and celebrated, here and there, quite often in fact, as God-infused, as sacred.

Theology at the hospice, as that study concerned the nature of God, dissolved in the fixed eyes, hollow faces, and skeletal remains of Wayne, Jesse, Sarah, Don, Laura, Ted, and hundreds and hundreds of others. Among such sorrow, suffering, and trauma, we could not find a way to let a theistic, unmoved mover God off the hook. We could not save God by ascribing to God the role of innocent bystander, who gives humanity the freedom to make

---

[24] I first presented my reflections on God and the Hospice at Mission Hill in Blaine-Wallace, "A Pastoral Psychology of Lament," 131–37.

its own bed. Nor, though I tried, could we reason that, horrified at history after the likes of the Holocaust, God turned away from our history, disowned us. In all cases God lost God's license to be God. Theology at the hospice petered out as a systematic study and emerged as an ethic.

The stewardship of the ethic was simple: learned regard for and emerging awareness of the sacredness of the other. Ronnie was from Mission Hill's initial community of mostly white, urban gay men. Johnny was one of the first to come to Mission Hill from another community, the straight, poor black community. Ronnie and Johnny became fast friends. Their initial bond was a shared struggle to breathe, each having virulent bouts of *Pneumocystis carinii* pneumonia, a disease common to persons with AIDS. Johnny's and Ronnie's friendship was foundational to softening the fear, increasing the curiosity about, and dissolving the relational distance between the two tribes. Still, Johnny did not cotton to Barbra Streisand or appreciate the Mapplethorpe prints in the common area, nor Ronnie the "loud noise" of Ice-T. At Mission Hill the other remained the other—impenetrable, unknowable, not to be merged with or consumed by neighbor. Mikhail Bakhtin writes:

> Only love can see and represent the inner freedom of an object. . . . The absolute unconsumability of the object is revealed only to love; love leaves it whole and situated outside of itself and side by side with itself.[25]

What of the God who suffers with us, who accompanies us through our suffering? At Mission Hill we relationally held onto and felt the presence of what I know to be and name the vulnerable, expendable God mirrored in the maligned and executed Jesus and the Father made crazy by the Son's execution. Still, this

---

[25] In Ruth Coates, *Christianity and the Exiled Author* (New York: Cambridge University Press, 1998), 175.

God was rarely identified and named. Who has the right to utter the name of the suffering God? South African theologian Denise Ackerman writes:

> Was God in the gas ovens when Jewish children were thrown into them alive, or with Tutsis slaughtered by machetes or with babies dying slowly of AIDS in hospital wards? Perhaps. I don't know. What is clear to me is that one's affirmation that God is present in suffering must, in Ken Surin's words, be "interrupted by the stories of the victims." They must speak just as loudly as any affirmations of faith about God's presence in suffering.[26]

I do preach/witness a lot about God pushed out of the world and onto the cross, but only to "Christians." I justify my Christian offerings as those verified by the hospice community and certified by them as sharable with my tribe. I did not earn the authority to witness—authority was bestowed.

The God of the hospice is less the steward of dialogue and more the one who disappears into dialogue like a great author exiled to the Patmos[27] of his or her own creative genius, silenced by his or her own adroitly effacing hand. What if *The Brothers Karamazov* wrote Dostoyevsky? The God of the hospice stands in opposition to the lesser author whose presence hovers over the text by asserting himself or herself in, under, around, and through the characters.[28]

The God of the hospice was all-pervasive. At the hospice God had no isolated essence and consciousness apart from the polyphonic music that was Jesse, in his sequined, gold gown, with thick,

---

[26] Denise Ackerman, *After the Locusts: Letters from a Landscape of Faith* (Grand Rapids, MI: Eerdmans, 1978), 106–7.

[27] The Greek island where the disciple John is said to have written Revelation.

[28] See Ralph C. Wood, "Flannery O'Connor's Preachers and Mikhail Bakhtin's Dialogical Understanding of Truth," *Flannery O'Connor Review* 1 (2001): 6.

turquoise eye liner, holding the hand of the by-now-blind Sally, describing, in rich detail, how beautiful he was at the moment, how great he was at being her eyes, while the rest of the residents in the room exclaimed, "Don't you believe that gaudy-assed girly man, Sally. Don't you believe it!" They were composing God.

God is incarnated, dies, and is resurrected in a particular dialogic relation of a few fellow hospice sufferers hanging out for a few moments. These few fellow sufferers acted as the silent and pervasive God of the hospice acts,

> orchestrating an open-ended conversation among [one another], as their lives and voices interact within the great polyphony of human existence, refusing to impose any truth than that which emerges from their own developing consciousness amidst the hazards of interpersonal life.[29]

The residents of the hospice mostly deconstructed, rather than trashed, religion. Wayne still reverenced the crucifix on the wall facing his bed. Richard read his bible. Sarah insisted on grace at the table. The residents desired more of the yet-to-be named or fully known God, faintly glimpsed during a game of dominoes or at breakfast. They experienced and imagined enough radical, boundless conviviality to utter their own, unique doxologies. The residents *did church*. Moreover, the emptied symbols and rote doctrines they brought to the hospice sometimes came back to life, having been infused with relation.

The God of the hospice is captured by Henry James Sr. in his words about Ralph Waldo Emerson:

> This was Emerson's incontestable virtue to everyone who appreciated him, that he recognized no God outside himself

---

[29] Ibid.

and his interlocutor, and recognized him there only as the liaison between the two, taking care that all their intercourse should be holy with a holiness undreamed of before by man or angel.[30]

The extended hands of emaciated wherewithal and hunger for connection was the hospice's fount of divine energy.

## The Season of Absence

Since my decade-long *metanoia* from belief to faith, I've added a season to my liturgical calendar: Ascension Day to the Day of Pentecost. During these ten days, and in regard to the historic church's three-tier universe, the risen Christ goes up to heaven in a cloud on Ascension Day, now at one with the Father, and the Holy Spirit comes down to earth on the Day of Pentecost like a fiery asteroid. We are thus alone for the ten days in between.

The season of absence is a homecoming, a reunion. I invite those from my past and present who have had to make God when they were left to themselves without God: those who have had to conjure the trinitarian dance for themselves; those who know so much more about Holy Saturday than either Good Friday or Easter Sunday; those who, isolated together in hell, find a way to exist, who, according to theologian Shelly Rambo, painstakingly seek a "weary trickle of love" that may flow "toward life."[31]

Those who died in the Grady hospice program and at the Hospice at Mission Hill without God or family are on my invitation list. Gregory wondered if he would live long enough to celebrate his twenty-sixth birthday, three weeks away. His wish was that

---

[30] *The Literary Remains of the Late Henry James*, edited with an introduction by William James (Boston: Houghton, Mifflin and Company, 1897).

[31] Shelly Rambo, *Spirit and Trauma: A Theology of Remaining* (Louisville, KY: Westminster John Knox Press, 2010), 152.

he would, even though he was very tired. His desire was that his parents would drive up from Savannah to celebrate with him. He feared that if he asked them, they would not come. They would find another excuse. After Gregory and I talked through his desire, he decided not to ask. He said that he could not bear another rejection. A few of us shared cake and ice cream with Gregory several days later, in case he died before his birthday.

Robert usually comes to my reunion also. When Robert was dying, the hospice physician and I were at his bedside in the hospital. Robert's father nervously paced in and out of the hospital room. When Robert died, the father begged the physician to change the cause of death on the death certificate, saying that if their retirement community found out their son had AIDS, they might lose many of their friends.

My first few years celebrating the season of absence, I invited my mainline Christian friends to join us. Not many showed up. Their excuses were similar to that of a good friend back in the day, a church friend. We were at an Atlanta Symphony concert. The first half of the concert was a work commissioned in 1946 by the Atlanta Symphony in memory of Franklin Roosevelt, *When Lilacs Last in the Dooryard Bloom'd*, based on a poem of the same name by Walt Whitman. The poem is an elegy that lifts up the horrors of the Civil War. My friend said, "Only Bill appreciates this gloom and doom. I'm out of here!"

The season of absence has a patron saint—Bonhoeffer, of course—who writes:

> The God who is with us is the God who forsakes us (Mark 15:34). The God who lets us live in the world with the working hypothesis of God is the God before whom we stand continually. Before God and with God we live without God.[32]

---

[32] Bonhoeffer, *Letters and Papers from Prison*, 360.

And the season of absence has music: Bach Cantata 11, the Ascension Oratorio. The cantata begins and ends with rather glorious choruses. The choruses, to me, feel dry, bright, and linear. But Bach's heart opens in the space between the choruses. It is as if he is redeeming himself for succumbing to the much less Lutheran beginning and ending. The translation of the bass recitative reads:

> Ah, Jesus, is Your departure already so near?
> Ah, is the hour then already there
> When we must let You leave us?
> Ah, behold, how hot tears
> Roll down our pale cheeks,
> How we yearn after You,
> How all our consolation is nearly destroyed.
> Ah, do not withdraw from us yet!

And the alto aria that follows:

> Ah, just stay, my dearest Life,
> Ah, don't flee so soon from me!
> Your farewell and Your early departure
> Brings me the greatest of all sorrows,
> Ah, truly, just stay awhile here;
> Otherwise I will be completely undone with grief.[33]

The true church is bracketed by the historic church's theology of glory. We need to make more music.

This chapter completes Part I. In Part II our focus is more practical. We focus on how to create and sustain lamentational relation in the communities to which we belong.

---

[33] Translations of the bass recitative and alto aria are from the website of Emmanuel Music, which provides notes for and translations of all the Bach cantatas.

## PART II

## GOING ON TOGETHER

*Above the hotel gate, I saw a sign:*
*"International Conference on Inflammation of the Eye"*
*for those who have cried too much or not cried enough.*
*All of them with name tags on their lapels*
*like temporary nameplates in a cemetery or markers*
*in a botanical garden.*
*They approach one another as if sniffing, as if checking,*
*Who are you where are you from and when*
*was the last time you cried?*
*The subject of the morning session is "Sobbing:*
*The end of Crying or the Way It Begins." Sobbing*
*as soul-stuttering and griefstones. Sobbing*
*as a valve or a loop that links cry to cry,*
*a loop that unravels easily, like a hair ribbon,*
*and the crying—hair that fans out in profusion, glorious.*
*Or a loop that pulls into an impossible knot—*
*sobbing like an oath, a testimony, a cure.*
*Back in their cubicles, the women translators are busy*
*translating fate to fate, cry to cry. At night they come home,*

*scrub the words from their lips, and with sobs of happiness
they start loving, their eyes aflame with joy.*
—YEHUDA AMICHAI, "OPEN CLOSED OPEN"

*I*n Part I we imagined and examined biblical, theological, ecclesiological, sociological, and psychological dimensions of lament in the context of a democratic capitalism that is increasingly less democratic. In Part II we focus less on inquiry and more on application.

In the spirit of Yehuda Amichai's poem, we *convene* in order to learn how to create space, conditions, and contexts that enable our tears to make a more resonant and joyous song. In Chapter 5 we explore how the constant and immediate news of the world's horrors overwhelm, blunt, and agitate our hearts. We examine how we might keep our hearts open and engaged with the world in our face. In Chapter 6 we examine seven dynamics of lament-based relation: silence, listening, alterity, hospitality, reiteration, marking absence, and curiosity. In Chapter 7 we learn a concrete way for parishes and communities to steward lamentational relation. In Chapter 8 we examine a parish that from its inception has privileged lamentational relation as the heartbeat of its life together. We distill from our examination four characteristics of lament that shape Christian community.

## 5

# World in Our Face

## *Daily Horrors*

Otto Warmbier, the University of Virginia student arrested while in North Korea and released to his parents after seventeen months in captivity only to die several days later, is, ten months later, back at the center of my consciousness. Yesterday, I witnessed again the scene of his agonizing wail at the reading of the guilty verdict and subsequent march out of the North Korean courtroom. The occasion of this new visitation is the public response to President Trump's assent to Kim Jong-un's assertion that he did not know of the Warmbier situation.

When tears sing, hearts are opened. Open hearts are more susceptible to the pain in, around, and beyond us. Lamentational communities are challenged, as spiritual teacher Ram Dass reminds us, "to keep our hearts open in the hurricane."[1] How do we keep our hearts alive in a hurting world that breaks through filters that keep us from being overwhelmed? Confession and prayer keep us more vulnerable to and available for the world-the-way-it-really-is.

---

[1] Ram Dass often used this phrase when working with the staff of the Hospice at Mission Hill.

## Confession

*60 Minutes*, CBS's news documentary, aired a story on April 8, 2018, about Bryan Stevenson's mission to visit the sites of lynchings. During the segment, graphic photographs of the lynching victims were aired. CBS, knowing the photographs would disturb some viewers and offend others, prepared a related story on the *60 Minutes* website about why it chose to air the photographs. Its argument is that such an abominable part of our history does not need to be forgotten or "softened." What is the value, in regard to lament-infused relation, of witnessing a postcard with a burned and mutilated corpse on the front and a little boy writing, on the back, "This is the barbeque we had last night!"?

This postcard and other photos, like the one of Jesse Washington tortured and hung at a community lynching in Waco, Texas, with thousands in attendance, one man hoisted on another man's back so he could see, bring us to our grounding confession. Waco is Golgotha. Jesse Washington is our God. We confess that the tortured and immolated young man on the postcard is the suffering Other, who determines us and our life in community. And what about *60 Minutes'* 2004 exposé of photographs of American soldiers humiliating and torturing prisoners at Abu Ghraib prison in Iraq? The photo of a hooded prisoner draped in black, electrical wires extending from his hands, standing on a block of wood in cruciform position is eerily Christlike. *Crucify him. Crucify him.*

The grotesque helps reveal God to somnolent hearts. God is exposed by those and that which are radically incongruent with a culture that worships the intact and sufficient self. To turn away from that which we objectify as gross, out of disgust and offense, knowingly or unwittingly, is in the service of a housebroken faith. We embody Flannery O'Connor's indictment: We have learned to "domesticate despair and live with it happily."[2]

---

[2] Flannery O'Connor, *Mystery and Manners: Occasional Prose,* selected and edited by Sally and Robert Fitzgerald (New York: Noonday, 1970), 159.

Belden Lane, in his enduring book *The Solace of Fierce Landscapes*, offers three perspectives from which to engage prayerfully with the grotesque.[3] First, the grotesque helps us see that God rarely presents as a gentle persuasion to change. God, at times, breaks through, cracks open, and assaults. At times my path to wholeness is not found or forged. It's laid bare. Whether or not I follow is another thing.

I remember Ruby Turpin, the disturbingly sweet Christian lady in Flannery O'Connor's short story "Revelation." Ruby wasn't really slain by the Holy Spirit until a surly, tormented freshman, Mary Grace, back home in the Deep South for the summer after her first year at Wellesley College, sits across from Ruby in a doctor's waiting room. Mary Grace, no longer able to handle an incessantly yakking and saccharine Ruby, throws a human development textbook at Ruby's head and shouts, "Go back to hell where you came from, you old warthog!"[4]

Flannery's mother once asked Flannery if she might write something pleasant that people would like. Flannery answered best in her essay titled "Mystery and Manners": "To the hard of hearing you shout, and for the almost blind you draw large and startling figures."[5]

Second, the grotesque clarifies what it means to be more fully human. Photographer Diane Arbus writes, "There is a quality of legend about freaks, like a person in a fairy tale who stops you and demands that you answer a riddle."[6]

In Boston, while I was serving Emmanuel Church, Bobby often stopped me and demanded that I answer a question about

---

[3] Belden Lane, *The Solace of Fierce Landscapes: Exploring Desert and Mountain Spirituality* (New York: Oxford University Press, 1998), 32–36.

[4] Flannery O'Connor, *The Complete Stories* (New York: Farrar, Straus and Giroux, 1971), 500.

[5] O'Connor, "Mystery and Manners," in O'Connor, *Mystery and Manners*, 34.

[6] Diane Arbus, *Diane Arbus* (New York: Museum of Modern Art, 1972), 3. As cited in Lane, *The Solace of Fierce Landscapes*, 33.

what it means to be human. Bobby, a young man with physical deformities, sold soft drinks from his wheelchair situated in front of the Burberry boutique, across the street from the church. Bobby could not manage his hands, so I'd fetch my drink from his cooler and give him a dollar. Bobby loved the Red Sox. He listened to the games on a transistor radio. Sometimes I took in a few minutes of the game with him. I'd shout and he'd slur, "Yankees suck, Yankees suck." We'd keep at it until the crowd chimed in.

Burberry. Our culture substitutes the glamorous for the grotesque, mostly from fear of impermanence. Our understanding of what is human often precludes damaged and deranged forms. People with long-term chronic and terminal disease often disappear into loneliness because they no longer possess what we assume to be the chief marks of human value—beauty and strength.

Third, the grotesque reforms the way we imagine the Divine. The grotesque dares me to submit my faith to the test of my late grandmother lying in a bed at the county home. Nanny stared at who knows what, breakfast egg hardened on her chin, smelling of urine and feces, false teeth resting in cloudy water on the metal bed stand, unmoved by the old man screaming his lungs out across the hall.

I ask myself, my sense of the suffering God reflected on in the last chapter having evaporated in the hell of the moment: Can my God cut it at a bedside like Nanny's? Can my God resist reciting the Twenty-third Psalm, mumbling a prayer, and racing out the door to the Fat Tuesday pancake supper, a pastoral duty accomplished? I've done that. Nanny represents the God from whom I am sometimes tempted to flee and other times moved to touch. Moved to touch when Nanny at the county home and I are more like than unlike.

### Prayer

How do we transpose wailing born of the horror of the lynching postcard into an emergent "peace that passes all understanding"? How do we pray resurrection in the face of the grotesque? If we confess that Otto Warmbier and the cruciform prisoner in Abu Ghraib are our embodied God, lament-based prayer is at the foot of a taunted and tortured God. How do we pray terror, revulsion, and dread?

Often our first inclination is to console. We imagine that godly prayer for a God in distress are prayers that quiet God's agony and fear. Such prayer, I find, is not as selfless as it seems. If God feels better, I feel better. Lament-based prayer is a call to something more than comforting God, and, by extension, ourselves. We are summoned to grittier prayer. Prayer before the suffering God harkens back to the heart of lamentational relation. Testifier and witness. God testifies. We witness.

The lamentational covenant, as the biblical Lamentations reminds us, requires that we sit on our beneficent hands in order that we do not silence the suffering God and soothe ourselves, the disquieted listener. Faithfulness to the covenant subverts beneficence for the sake of God's comfort and ours. Through covenantal fidelity, the evolution of suffering love—agitated and agitating toward restoration and renewal—is not thwarted. The ache and anguish of God, undomesticated, is that which reaches toward Zion. The hand of lament-based prayer is eschatological, agonizingly stretching toward the future.

A difficult question: How do we stay in a witnessing position when all hell is breaking loose in and around God and our world? How do we remain hopeful? I have come to trust five expressions of lament-based prayer that enliven lamentational relation: refract; be still; wait patiently; stay curious; and cloak suffering.

Before investigating these expressions, I give attention to currents that pull us away from lament-based prayer.

## Rant, Judgment, and Embodied Pain

*Outrage is strange bait: It can feel wrong not to take it.*
—SALVATORE SCIBONA,
"THE INDUSTRIAL REVOLUTION OF SHAME"

We are tempted to flee the grotesque. By flee, I mean closing our hearts to life-the-way-it-really-is. Closed hearts make noise. We rant. I remember a cover of *The Lutheran* magazine, some forty years ago, with a shiny red Christmas ornament at center. Transposed onto the ornament's reflection was a photograph of a starving child. The letters to the editor howled at the cover. "Can't we have one day of the year to ourselves, Christmas Day, without the pain of the world shoved in our face?!"

We judge. Jesmyn Ward's 2011 National Book Award–winning novel, *Salvage the Bones,* follows a poor black family's journey through the days leading up to, during, and following Hurricane Katrina. The book portrays the ravages of poverty with stark, unnerving clarity.  At times I had to work hard to keep reading, a reaction echoed in several Amazon reviews. Several reviewers could not get through the book, unable to bear or connect with the misery. Other reviewers seemed to flirt with the desire to tell the characters to get a life, enough already! We who are self-sufficient are tempted to keep our distance from and blame those who are drastically reliant. We objectify the poor. When we construct the poor as "depraved," we hide, or are made blind to, that which poverty steals from persons—their humanity.

Paul LePage, past governor of Maine, fails to accept or understand the difference between the insidious despair of systemic poverty and episodic, situational poverty. When in office Governor

LePage crowed, as often as he could, about his rise above poverty. On the streets as a teenager due to a violent father and broken home, he fought his way into college and up the ladder.

Paul LePage has no tolerance for those who "lie on the couch all day in front of the TV," a trope he loved to drag into many a speech. He vowed to help only those who helped themselves. Mr. LePage's judgment against the poor echoes the chants of "welfare queens," a trope at the heart of President Reagan's presidential campaign. The reality that poverty is rooted less in the character of poor people and more in the monetary, political, and bigoted underbelly of our society escapes Mr. LePage.

Moreover, our culture is in the throes of an epidemic of judgment. A good friend of mine during my undergraduate years was in a fraternity. I, older and already married, was not. Over the years my friend has made a great difference for the good in terms of his vocation and commitments to community. He embraces progressive movements. He is an active Democrat. As a result of his public service he is well known in the community. A reporter for the local paper found a yearbook photo of his fraternity, over three decades ago. My friend was one of about one hundred undergraduates gathered around a Confederate flag. A recent photo of my friend and the fraternity photo were published side by side.

Salvatore Scibona writes:

> We are undergoing an industrial revolution in shame. New technologies have radically expanded our ability to make and distribute a product. The product is our judgment of one another. As in past industrial revolutions, the mass manufacture and use of a product previously available to just a few or in small amounts has given us the power to do harm at a previously unthinkable scale. . . . The defendants carted into the virtual crossroads are public figures as well as previously inconspicuous people—a drunk in a parking lot, a girl who

overshares on Instagram. One day an actor is accused of faking a hate crime, another day a politician admits he attended a dance contest wearing blackface, another day a high school student's grin seems to embody the contemptuous privilege of his class, another day those describing his grin that way are shamed for shaming him on preliminary evidence. To bring up any one of these examples is to invite the objection, "That time it was deserved!" Maybe so. But is there no way of discussing these controversies that doesn't come down to whether an offender deserved the punishment?[7]

Scibona suggests that we consider moving from the jury box to the witness chair:

> Too often we may feel ourselves trapped in the jury box, but we put ourselves there, and we can choose instead to sit in the chair of the witness. Freed from the responsibility to deliver a verdict, our new role is to separate assumption from knowledge. Watching this way, whether on the page or on the street, releases us from the tyranny of our own estimations, even regarding people who have behaved in ways we might otherwise consider wicked. . . . It is a no less morally awake response than holding a person in judgment.[8]

Rant and judgment are the louder ways we close our hearts to the more grotesque wailings of the sorrowful, suffering, and traumatized. Subtler and harder to identify is the manner in which we guard our hearts from the terror of the world brought often and near to our daily lives. We embody the pain. Embodiment manifests as anxiety, fear, boredom, anger, aimlessness, busyness, and substance

---

[7] Scibona, "The Industrial Revolution of Shame," *New York Times*, Opinion, March 9, 2019.

[8] Ibid.

abuse. We wail daily, and to a degree that makes it extremely hard to transform our inarticulate, muted, numb utterances of disquietedness into lament. We are too wired to slow down, too numb to wake up, too distracted to attend to the moment, too hungry to listen to our bodies, too confused to pray our lives and relations.

The following expressions of lament-based prayer help curb my tongue, quicken my spirit, calm my body, and keep my heart more open than not.

## Refract

The terrors of our lives and world are stark. Like a stained-glass window, which bends light into colors and configurations that bless, we do well to bend the more intense glare of fear, dread, and pain into shades that allow us to feel, name, and engage a broken world.

Our daughter miscarried this week. Sarah Frances sent a text last night. She thanked me for reaching out. She shared that she wanted to respond but did not know what to say. She said that she could not find words to express the sadness, and that she would respond when words came. I texted back saying that when I'm in the midst of pain too large to bear, pain that outruns words, I often approach the pain through hymns—just the tune, no words. Music, for me and maybe Sarah Frances, transposes the noise of immediate loss and sorrow into sounds that bless. I sent Sarah Frances Chris Rice's offering of "Fairest Lord Jesus" from his album *The Living Room Sessions*.

Last week a friend and I saw the movie *They Shall Not Grow Old*, a stirring documentary about World War I. The movie consists of original footage of trench warfare using modern reproduction techniques. Nothing more. The story of what was arguably the deadliest and most gruesome modern-era war was offered by the voices of those who experienced it, the foot soldiers. Their voices and dialogues put the immense carnage of human remains and

horse carcasses into a relational context that kept me from darting
out the door.

Art keeps me curious and prayerfully awake to the surreal underbelly of history. Art bends terror into color, shades, and stories
that we can stomach in the service of a heart open in the hurricane. Caravaggio, Goya, Kafka, Munch, Flannery O'Connor's short
stories, and Jasmyn Ward's award-winning novels refract suffering
into dimensions I can prayerfully hold. Picasso's *Guernica* has had
a place in my study for forty years. I pray the leveled town of
Aleppo, Syria, through a painting by fifteenth-century German
artist Albrecht Altdorfer titled *The Birth of Christ*. Mary and Joseph,
the infant Jesus, and three mysteriously jolly angels (what did those
cherubs know?) are holed up in the basement of an abandoned,
gutted-out edifice. Only part of the facade remains. The ground
underneath the holy family, barn animals, and angels is barren
save weeds creeping up and around splintered timbers tentatively
holding up a very uncertain ceiling. The disturbing chill is not as
emotionally frigid as new footage of Aleppo offered on the PBS
*News Hour* last night.

On my desk I have a photograph of a young girl, about ten,
posing beside a loom in a western North Carolina cotton mill. The
photograph helps me pray the daily grind I imagine my ancestors
endured in the eastern North Carolina cotton mills.

## Be Still

Being still does not mean staying still. Sometimes there is motion
to stillness. Last spring I was particularly melancholic, more than
the usual doldrums that accompany mud season in Maine. I walked
our labyrinth in the orchard. The walks were unremarkable. The
experience was more like meandering through the hay mazes that
populate my region of Maine around Halloween. Kids are amazed;
parents endure. During my morning meditations, sitting per usual

in the chair in my study, my mind had a more difficult time dropping into my heart.

One afternoon, later in May, I was on my riding lawn mower mowing the grass between the paddock and orchard. The yard is bordered by a very large pasture. When finished, with little forethought, and surprising myself, I turned the lawn mower toward the pasture. I meandered about, making a path of aimless turns, bends, intersections, ending where I began. I created a walking path. The walk takes about thirty minutes. About ten yards into the path I hung from an apple tree a wood plank inscribed with Mary Oliver's poem "Summer Day" on one side and on the other side Laura Gilpin's poem "Two-Headed Calf." On small pieces of old lumber I wrote one word on each: love, beauty, silence, sad, angry, forgive, peace, joy, curiosity, attention, gratitude, relation. On my daily, sometimes twice-daily walks, I often paused before whatever word or words caught my attention and pertained to the moment. After about a month I removed the words. I no longer needed them to connect my heart to who and what matters. Walking was enough to pray my life and the world the way they really are. Sometimes, when meeting with a couple stuck in blame and shame (my practice is on the farm), I send them to the path with only one requirement. Silence.

Prayerful contemplation is whatever slows down, stills, and opens our hearts to who and what matters.

## Wait Patiently

The Rothko Chapel, in Houston, Texas, is an austere space. A caption on the Rothko Chapel website captures the spirit of the space: "A Stillness that Moves." Recently, during an initial meeting with someone I now meet with for spiritual direction, the person shared that she had recently visited the chapel. My ears perked up. Forty years ago, during an intense internship year in Houston, I often visited the chapel as a place of refuge. My new friend's description of the chapel left me feeling as if I had prayed there yesterday.

She mentioned that when she first sat in the chapel, nothing happened. She shared that after a while the space opened up and drew her in. I shared that my first experience there was similar.

What if the chapel had failed to draw us in? Possibly we were ahead of the curve. The chapel did its duty on the first visit. If it had not, would I have left saying, "So what? What's the big deal? Rothko's paintings are really bleak!" I probably would not have said that. I love his work.

We expect too much from prayerful contemplation. We expect prayerful contemplation to adhere to our culture's restitution narrative. Deliver the goods or else. Good luck. A crucified God is not in a position to make us feel or do better on our clock.

As I write, I am back in the South, a few hours from attending one of my favorite cousin's memorial service. He suicided a week ago, a few days after my daughter miscarried. After arriving yesterday, and before checking into the hotel, I visited my mother, who still lives in an assisted-living center. She has end-stage Alzheimer's. She was having one of the days when not only did she not know me, she was not in a place where she could welcome anyone. I lasted fifteen minutes. Why did I expect Mom to show up for me? I know better than to expect that.

Lament-based prayer is on God's time. Not ours. Advent is the season of such prayer. Waiting—but waiting patiently, not waiting "until." Until what? I find that waiting for something from God until it is received, when it is received, often is issued from a heart less wounded than God's. Waiting, just waiting beside Mom/God, God/Mom, waiting beyond my needs and desires opens up possibilities of love heretofore unimagined and never captured. Love offered from the wounded heart of God is evolutionary. This love expands beyond our grasp and comprehension, moving out of arm and heart's reach, progressing toward and in service to a bigger love.

## Stay Curious

Waiting patiently, like being still, is in the active voice. Waiting patiently summons us to prayer grounded in a curiosity that questions its way past assumptions and expectations, in other words, past our prayer agendas. Waiting curiously helps contain the fear, repulsion, and terror that are evoked by the cruciformed in our midst. One question after another, no questions that I already know or think I might know the answer to. Questions that keep me in a *not knowing* position, a position that creates newer and unfolding knowledge (a position we explore in the next chapter).

I wish I could retrieve my fifteen minutes with Mom/God, God/Mom. Mom/God, God/Mom, you looked at your hand, turned it this way and that as if you were exploring it. Does it hurt? If your hand could speak, what would it say to you, to me? Did your hand help protect you from Dad's rage more or less than I imagine? May I slip my hand into yours? Yours into mine? What do you feel holding my hand? What am I feeling holding yours? Your flat affect? I wonder if they overmedicated you today. They say that you often get anxious if you aren't sedated enough. What do you get anxious about? Are you sometimes afraid? Of what? Coming through the corridor a while ago, I saw the nursing assistant who pays special attention to you. How does she calm you down? Does she make you feel safer? My sister, Bebe, do you remember her? Bebe said that last week, out of the blue, you called my name. You told Bebe that I was stylish. What do you mean by that? What about these jeans, my flannel shirt, and my rubber and leather boots that are all the rage up where I live? What do you think?

Staying curious opens up relational space between testifier and witness, between the heart of the suffering God and us.

## Cloak Suffering

Novelist Elizabeth Strout introduces readers to tall and ruddily handsome Tyler Caskey, beloved pastor of a congregational church in rural Maine in 1959. Tyler has lost his wife to cancer, a wife less loved by the congregation than Tyler but tolerated. A year into the loss Tyler has not regained his bearings. From the pulpit, at coffee hour, during meetings, which, in the past, were platforms for his gentle authority, Tyler feels like "a big tractor being driven by a teenage kid, slipping in and out of gear."[9]

The failure of his five-year-old daughter to thrive is his greatest ache. Her pain, a muted and clinging wail that has rattled the kindergarten class, especially the teacher, rests just below his neck bone. It is like "a small rodent who lives inside him, clinging with tiny-needled claws."[10] Tyler, unlike Thomas, does not need to see and touch the wound in the side of Jesus. Lately, Tyler embodies it.

I imagine each of us now and again has an enfleshed inkling of the spear mark. I do, each year on my birthday, May 22. The pain, some fifty-seven years old, does not abate. Walking up the front steps of the porch, just home from school, I find Mom weeping, a few decibels short of sobbing. She points and says, "There's your birthday present." I open it. It is not the baseball glove I asked for. It is a thin representation of it. More dime than sporting goods store. I tear up and rush inside.

Here's a pain I still can't parse. Mom's? Mine? Whose was the worst? Mom's it seems. And what's mine worth? And why indulge it? What about the kids in the neighborhood of Sarah, the domestic

---

[9] Elizabeth Strout, *Abide with Me* (New York: Random House, 2007), 97.
[10] Ibid., 29.

worker in my childhood home? Her kids' sports equipment was sticks and cans. My ache is more a catch in the back of my throat.

A while back, while making my way through a local art gallery, I saw a weaving. Wool. Black and royal blue threads woven into a two-by-six-foot piece. Is it a wall hanging or a shawl? For me, a shawl. I bought it. Most mornings I wrap it around my shoulders and sit for prayer. Shrouding my ache keeps my mind from trying to understand it, my heart from softening it, my conscience from legitimizing it. Sorrow, suffering, trauma wrapped in deep-hued love opens me to a love that is local and cosmic, particular and universal.

Tyler, having come through the front door after an exhausting meeting with his daughter's kindergarten teacher, is greeted by the housekeeper:

> The minister stood in his long coat, his big shoulders slightly hunched. He dropped the car keys on the coffee table. "How did it go?" The minister didn't answer. But when he met the eyes of his housekeeper, he had one of those surprising moments that occur sometimes, when there's a fleeting sense of recognition, when, in less than half a second, there's the sense of having glimpsed the other's soul, some shred of real agreement being shared. This is what happened to the minister on that autumn evening, the walls of the living room now a dull, flat pink. *It's a sad world*, the housekeeper's eyes seemed to say. *And I'm sorry.* The minister's eyes said, *It is a sad world, isn't it. I'm sorry, too.*[11]

Being cloaked in love, regularly, opens our hearts wider for lamentational relation, allowing us to see more fully the eternal now that beholds us.

---

[11] Ibid., 30–31.

## Prayers of the Tortured and Terrorized

What about Otto Warmbier and the cruciform prisoner at Abu Ghraib? How did they pray? Or the spooned-together "inventory" of the slave trade traveling through the Middle Passage across the Atlantic Ocean from Africa?

In North America and most first-world societies, prayer is that which we decide to do, a practice we work to stay faithful to. Not so for the tortured and terrorized. They discover and embrace prayer *in extremis* and toward survival.

Barbara A. Holmes writes:

Contemplation usually occurs at the leisure of the one who has the freedom to decide how to enter into the divine presence. It is purportedly the epitome of peace and repose. However, contemplation can also be a displacement of the ordinary, a paradigm shift that becomes a temporary refuge when human suffering reaches the extent of spiritual and psychic dissolution. It can be a state of extraordinary spiritual attenuation, a removal to a level of reality that allows distance from excruciating circumstances.[12]

Holmes imagines the moans of the children, women, and men shackled together in the bowels of the slave ships:

The moan stitches horror and survival instincts into a creation narrative, a tapestry of historical memory that marks the creation of community. On the slave ships, the moan became the language of stolen strangers, the sound of unspeakable fears, the precursor to joy yet unknown.[13]

---

[12] Barbara A. Holmes, *Joy Unspeakable: Contemporary Practices of the Black Church,* 2nd ed. (Minneapolis: Fortress Press, 2017), 50.

[13] Ibid., 52.

I imagine us, in our practices of lament-based prayer, inviting into our prayer space the prayerful testimonies of the tortured and terrorized, Otto Warmbier/God, God/Otto Warmbier, Jesse Washington/God, God/Jesse Washington, and the legions of the martyred and maligned who interrupt our daily lives and intentions. These prayer partners may teach us to rant and judge less, may empower us to name and address the ways we embody fear, repulsion, and dread. They may teach us to be better witnesses.

In the next chapter we explore that which is at the heart of the witnessing position—silence and listening—as well as ancillary ways to help us remain present with and for the testifying Other.

6

# Choir Rehearsal

## *Practicing Lament*

When I turn onto the private road of Emery House, the rural retreat of the Society of Saint John the Evangelist, an Episcopal monastery in Cambridge, Massachusetts, there is a yellow public street sign that reads *Slow*. Both cars and people slow down at Emery House. Slowing down the pace of our lives enables us to pay better attention to God. In this chapter we take a slower, more measured look at lamentational relation. We will learn how to create a relational space between persons that will generate a greater possibility for tears to sing.

The seven elements of lamentational relation, which I have come to trust as foundational, are silence, listening, alterity, hospitality, reiteration, marking absence, and curiosity.[1]

---

[1] I have written about the conversational qualities of lament in the following publications: "The Politics of Tears: Lamentation as Justice-Making," in *Injustice and the Care of Souls* (Minneapolis: Fortress Press, 2009): 183–97; "The Voice of Silence in Pastoral Conversation," *Journal of Pastoral Care and Counseling* 64, no. 1 (2010): 1–4; and "Post Christian Pastoral Care: The Wisdom of Not Knowing," *Journal of Pastoral Care and Counseling* 65, no. 2 (2011): 1–8.

## Silence

Silence has a passive voice.

Last winter my walking path slept under several feet of snow. Rudely, it seems, I crunch across it on snowshoes, shortest route possible, heading for the forest. Something like walking straight to, rather than circling toward, the center of a labyrinth. Once in the woods, I stop. The sleeping forest enfolds, a shawl of stillness and quiet. When my stillness lets too much of the cold through my clothing, I walk until I am warm again, and stop again. Snowshoeing is movement toward silences that bless.

Silence has an active voice.

Emma Gonzalez, a survivor of the Marjory Stone Douglas High School shooting in Parkland, Florida, stood silent on the stage for six and a half minutes at the March for Life rally against gun violence, tears streaming down her face—the amount of time it took the shooter to kill seventeen, and injure fifteen, of her fellow students. The then-state-representative from Maine, Mr. Leslie Gibson, responded to her tearful silence: "There is nothing about this skinhead lesbian that impresses me and there is nothing that she has to say unless you're a frothing-at-the-mouth moon bat." Ms. Gonzalez's silent tears rallied residents of Greene, Maine, to remove Mr. Gibson from the ballot in his reelection bid.

Mikhail Bakhtin writes that "in stillness there is no noise, while in silence there is a voice that does not speak."[2] In terms of lament, the "voice that does not speak" often is muted utterances torn from articulation and meaning by tragedy, violence, and loss. The voice is exiled. Emma Gonzalez's silent tears and those who witnessed them create a relational act of redeeming the banished utterance. The residents of Greene, Maine, liberated Gonzalez's exiled voice

---

[2] David Patterson, *Literature and Spirit: Essays on Bakhtin and His Contemporaries* (Louisville: University Press of Kentucky, 1988), 34.

to humanize a legislative district in Maine and the wider Maine community.

Respect for those who suffer imposes a silence.[3] Pastoral theologian Sharon Thornton writes that the place of silence at the feet of those who are grieving and aggrieved, when shed of professional trappings and contrivances and grounded in an open heart, is best described as a sacramental-like act of beholding.

Beholding is the beginning place of relation, prior to description and resistant to explanation, by which ordinary time is transposed into sacred moment. It is like the time, during Eucharist, when I as celebrant break the bread of God's broken body, hold the severed remains in two hands, and lift the pieces for the congregation to behold. The rubric in the *Episcopal Book of Common Prayer* reads, "A period of silence is kept." I think it more apt to say that an experience of silence is created.

Fundamental to stewarding a silence that beholds is an acknowledgment and respect for an inner voice, for what's going on inside mind and heart when in conversation, which participates in the conversational partnership. The inner voice of the witness does not wait to speak its mind, to move from the inner space to the outer world untouched and unscathed so that it can add its two cents to the dialogue. Rather, in respectful, curious conversation our internal reflections about what's going on in the conversation take shape and meaning as they are being offered, with a purpose to connect. Family therapist Harry Goolishian liked to say, "I do not know what I mean until I say it."[4] Words that take shape in the

---

[3] Sharon Thornton, *Broken Yet Beloved: A Pastoral Theology of the Cross* (St. Louis: Chalice Press, 2002), 204.

[4] In Harlene Anderson, "Dialogue: People Creating Meaning with Each Other and Finding Ways to Go On," in *Collaborative Therapy: Relations and Conversations That Make a Difference*, ed. Harlene Anderson and Diane Gehart (New York: Routledge, 2007), 39.

inner voice and find expression in conversation are the way testifier and witness go on together.

I begin my spiritual direction ministry and counseling practice in silence. The silence gives the testifier the space to find an utterance from his or her inner voice that brings shape to how the testifier desires for us to go on together for the next while. When there are moments when the words we are using cannot hold the meaning and depth of what's happening between us, we pause for silence. In the silence new utterances may emerge to move us along.

For several years I participated in a peer supervision group of pastoral counselors. We learned the importance of monitoring our conversations in regard to pace. Often we moved too fast in our offerings, not giving our inner voices time to shape our outer conversation. We knew we needed to slow down when we sounded like professional healers talking about our "patients." Slowing down created space for our inner curiosities, confessions, requests, and desires to take shape in service of going on together with those with whom we met. In the slower speaking of the words, we observe a birth of sorts. We unwrap gifts for purposeful conversation, conversation that connects and opens fresh space for the next movement in our relational dance.

When two people are in conversation, there are four voices: each person's inner and outer voices. Conversational partnership, I find, is less about reaching understanding and more about stewarding resonance among the four voices, a convivial timbre that augurs well for co-created meaning and possibility. I find that the more I think I know a conversational partner, the slower I need to go, because I am too quick to assume her steps. I step on her feet. Again, Harry Goolishian: "If you want to move quickly, go slowly."

Our inner voices are more disturbed and disquieted when we are listening to people who are sorrowful, suffering, and traumatized. We feel pressured to deliver words by express mail in order to help our neighbors. Our words toward caring do not have time to ferment and unfold in the dialogical space between us. Sometimes our inner voices may become horrified by what we are witnessing. Our tongues become more stuck than silent. The challenge is to leave our tongues stuck, resisting the temptation to pry them loose with words. Stuck tongues, as uncomfortable as they are, do respectfully behold. Usually, the respectfully beheld conversational partner, sensing our presence, offers utterances, in time, that loosen our tongue.

Furthermore, the grieving and aggrieved testifier, whose horrific experience leaves the witness speechless, struggles for words as well. The struggle is relative to the degree of the horror. The testifier struggles for utterances capable of conveying the nature and meaning of this horror. The search for utterances of meaning is harder in that the nature of the horror often is harder for the testifier to understand. The witness's silence, both offered and occasioned by the conversation, creates a space in which the testifier may convey more fully the horror of the experiences. Sometimes the witness's silence enables the testifier to restore exiled meaning or discover new meaning. Silence, then, is a co-creative action. If the testifier's experience fails to be conveyed or made meaning of, the witness's silence remains co-creative in that the testifier's space, which still may birth the not-yet-said, remains open because the witness has not closed the space with words.

A colleague and I interviewed Esperance, a survivor of the Rwandan genocide. She said that she did not know where to begin because words could not convey the horror of her experience. Nonetheless, she began and told a story of immense terror. Her one-year-old daughter was drowned in her presence. Her husband, parents, and siblings were butchered by machetes. After a two-hour testimony, during which I, the interviewer, offered only fifty-six words, Esperance shared her frustration at not being able to convey her experience or reflect on it in a meaningful way.

My colleague and I could have easily disagreed with that assessment. Rather, the three of us talked about the value of words even when words fall short of conveyance and meaning. We talked about how "failed" words serve to connect us in the midst of the indescribable and meaningless. My colleague said to me in Esperance's presence:

> You asked her, are you still looking for words? And I think words don't equal an explanation. They are just words, so
> . they are neither an explanation nor the experience that they refer to. Words are a way of building a community or a relationship among us, because what Esperance went through is something that will always remain foreign to me.

The inner voices of the three of us remained active after we left one another's company. When we are in lamentational conversation, our inner voices keep working after the conversations end. We struggle to find utterances that better convey and give meaning to the testifying-witnessing relation we shared. Our inner voices keep the conversation going, enriching the next conversation we have together. If we don't meet again, the knowledge received from our inner voices that continue after our conversation may well serve other and new conversational partnerships.

The inner voices in conversational partnership that continue the dialogue between and after meetings are receiving more attention in the therapy world. Narrative therapists encourage letter writing between meetings. The therapist practices "near-experience writing," lifting up particular words from the last meeting that have stirred the inner voice of the therapist and inspired the inner voice of the therapist to find words with which to reach out.

As the previous few paragraphs suggest, sorrow, suffering, and trauma create a double bind. Testifiers strongly desire to convey and make meaning of their experience, while at the same time the experience makes it harder to find words. Likewise, witnesses feel the need for words with which to address the sufferer at the same time that words seem inadequate and unavailable. Hence, the act of lamenting requires greater space for silence, more attention to our inner voices, from which utterances will, may, or may not take shape. Whatever the case, what we know is that the movement from wailing to lament, through more silence than usual, takes time.

I received an email from an undergraduate at Bates College. Joel, who was from Zimbabwe, participated with me in a memoirs group. The email arrived six months after the last session of the group.

> Hello Bill. My classes are going well. I am really enjoying the good weather! I just wish things were better back home, but I can only pray. I am taking a writing class and it's quite engaging. I have been engaged in deep thoughts lately. Most of the stuff that would be difficult to talk about. Maybe it's because of the ongoing problems back home, or just that I have more time to think about stuff, sometimes it just brings me anger. I miss the memoirs group as we could have potentially shared our inner thoughts and fears. However, I was wondering if you would be available during the summer as I would like to take my steps to write out issues that burn within me. I appreciate that the memoirs group was open for us to share our deep thoughts but I could have said much more. I hope you can help me let the thoughts out (thinking of your probing yet temperate questions during the interviews of the memoirs). God Bless You. Joel

### Listening

Silence as respectful attention to our inner voices is not the prelude to talk, the hush before the rush of dialogue. Rather, silence is the spring from which those who are beheld find the fresh water of words to communicate their experience. Hence, silence is listening that watches and waits and receives what the others are able and willing to share.

Silence-infused listening is exemplified by my now-deceased colleague Tom Andersen's interaction with a family. A counselor had arranged for Tom to meet with him and the family. The counselor told Tom before the meeting that his work with the family was stuck, that there had been little movement over the last couple of sessions.

Six persons—three men, two women, and an adolescent boy, representing three generations of one family—sit in a semicircle with their counselor. Tom enters the counseling room to the sound of loud chatter. Tom sits with the family. The clamor increases, particularly the giggles of the thirteen-year-old grandson of the quietest person in the room—the grandfather, who sits to Tom's right. Tom sits still and silent among the clamor for what seems like a long time. Eventually, Tom says, almost in a whisper, "There is much noise." The decibels increase, especially the sniggers of the adolescent. Tom waits a while longer and then softly says, "I wonder, if noise could speak, what would noise have to say to us?" In a few moments the grandfather speaks: "Noise would say that we need to speak." A nervous laughter issues from the grandson. The grandfather continues: "There is much to talk about that is hard to talk about but needs to be talked about." An uncomfortable silence remains.

Tom, looking around, says, "Is this too hard to bring to words now? What do you think? Shall we talk or not?" The grandfather responds, "We must talk about my cancer. We can't avoid it any longer. Yes, it is very hard for me. I've been independent for as long as I can remember, able to be strong for others. Now, I am going to be dependent. I don't know how. We must talk." A breeze of relation moves through the room.

Tom watched and waited in silence as he sat among the six family members and the therapist. Tom's silence enabled him eventually to name respectfully that which those around him offered, incomprehensible wailing: "There is much noise." Tom's simple and sublime naming is rich with insights critical to the dynamic that moves incomprehensible wailing to convivial lament, toward joyful solidarity that liberates.

Harry Goolishian said, "Listen to what they really say, and not to what they really mean."[5] Goolishian's wisdom is spiced with Ludwig Wittgenstein's philosophy: "The aspects of things that are most important for us are hidden because of their simplicity and familiarity. One is unable to notice something because it is always before our eyes."[6]

Verbal expressions are not gleanings from internal constructs; they are social contributions, gifts for participating in bonds with others. "Expressions bewitch understanding, not vice versa,"[7] through listening that creates enough room for the expressions to be voiced to, or nearer to, completion.

As witnesses we sometimes feel compelled to get at and understand what the testifier means, as if our task is the deliverance of meaning. We accompany, God delivers. How often I have said things to the sorrowful, suffering, and traumatized because I believed I needed to say something that helped, make a contribution that counted for something. The listening vocation is, first and last, about relation, not liberation. Liberation is less goal and more grace, grace that emerges in relation.

Lament requires no experts. The words the grieving and aggrieved share with us are not to be adroitly mined but valued, cherished, and treasured, qualities born of an innate, "naive" curiosity.[8] To assume that words have hidden meaning requiring our

---

[5] Tom Andersen, *A Collaboration, What Some Call Psychotherapy: Bonds Filled of Expressions, and Expressions Filled of Meaning* (unpublished manuscript, 2002).

[6] Ludwig Wittgenstein, *Philosophical Fragments* (Oxford, UK: Blackwell Publishers, 1953), 129.

[7] Andersen, *A Collaboration, What Some Call Psychotherapy.*

[8] Gerald Monk, Gerald Winslade, Kathie Crocket, David Epston, eds., *Narrative Therapy in Practice: The Archaeology of Hope* (San Francisco: Jossey-Bass, 1997), 302.

excavation is to cross beyond the boundary of that which is offered, which is a violation of the other's spirit. Words are gifts, not clues. Harlene Anderson thickens the distinction between gift and clue in talking about particular qualities of listening, hearing, and speaking:

> Listen, hear, and speak as a learner. Be genuinely curious about the other. You must sincerely believe that you can learn something from them. Listen and respond with expressed interest in what the other person is talking about—their experiences, their words, their feelings, and so forth.
>
> Listen, hear, and speak to understand. Do not understand too quickly. Keep in mind that understanding is never-ending. Be tentative about what you think you might know. Knowing interferes with dialogue: it can preclude learning about the other, being inspired by them, and the spontaneity intrinsic to genuine dialogue. Knowing also risks increasing power differences.[9]

Gifts are to be opened. Recall that Tom says, "I wonder, if noise could speak, what would noise have to say to us?" And the grandfather answers, "Noise would say that we need to speak." The grandfather continues, "There is much to talk about that needs to be talked about but is hard to talk about." Tom respectfully checks with the family to see if it is okay to continue to open the gift. "Is this too hard to bring to words now? What do you think? Should we talk or not?" The grandfather concludes, "We must talk about my cancer."

The grandfather, I believe, did not come to the session or wait for a time in the session to say, "We must talk about my cancer." I imagine the grandfather did not know what he was going to say before he said it,[10] as if the "unsaid" already exists, waiting for its time, waiting to be noticed, discovered, or "unearthed" by the craft

---

[9] Anderson, "Dialogue," 40.
[10] Monk et al., *Narrative Therapy in Practice*, 6.

of the therapist.[11] The initially silent Tom, paying respectful attention to the noise of incomprehensible wailing, allowed those in the room to name the not-yet-known, and through such naming be heard to a voice of lament. The voice of lament was a new, previously unstoried narrative, co-constructed by therapists and family in solidarity, awakening a previously unimagined future ripe with fresher possibility.

The Reverend Glenda Hope talks about a "life stance of thankfulness" that waits for God's guidance in silence,[12] what Sharon Thornton suggested "we might call contemplative listening, a disciplined kind of listening in which we attempt to disregard any of our preconceived notions, theories, and hunches about someone and their experiences."[13]

Contemplative listening urges us to take a cautious position with respect to empathy.[14] Empathy presumes the possibility of knowing the other, and privileges the act of knowing the other. The assumption that we share an understanding with another as the result of a resonant connection may violate the space or particularity of the other. Contemplative listening "brackets empathy with a 'hermeneutic of suspicion'"[15] and invites us to participate with the grieving and aggrieved in co-creating the not-yet-known, an imaginative enterprise of restoring "dignity, freedom, and hope."[16] We are tempted to announce and celebrate empathy in dialogues that create connection and make a difference. I find it is wise to approach the empathy that emerges in conversational partnership gingerly, curiously, and silently. My experience is that empathy is an inner voice utterance that does not need to be spoken to be conveyed. Sometimes, when empathy is conveyed, there is a sense

---

[11] Jill Freedman and Gene Combs, *Narrative Therapy: The Social Construction of Preferred Realities* (New York: W. W. Norton, 1996), 44–45.

[12] In Thornton, *Broken Yet Beloved*, 201.

[13] Ibid.

[14] Ibid.

[15] Ibid.

[16] Ibid.

that conversational partners have "arrived." A premature celebration ensues. Momentum stalls.

## Alterity

*Alterity* means differentness, otherness. Alterity, as a relational position, serves as a "handle" to hold on to in conversational partnership to keep us from slipping away from positions of learning and curiosity and slipping into power over positions of expertise, knowing, and understanding. Alterity checks our penchant for empathy and our approach to empathy as one of the more essential characteristics of being present with another.

Alterity is important because those with a gift for listening—often those who have experienced suffering and continue to make meaning of their suffering—may presume that they are in a better position to relate to those who suffer. While the sense of being a "fellow struggler" motivates us for engaged accompaniment, "fellow struggler" is not a dominant relational position in regard to lament. As similar as our histories may be to the histories of those we are in conversational partnership with, respectful and attentive listeners remember that the grieving and aggrieved other is and will always be the other; different from us, hence, one before whom we remain expectant and open to being inspired, touched, amazed, awed, blessed, and changed.

The suffering other, beheld by us, addresses us as the Other, the embodiment of God, about whom we can know little and predict less. The Other addresses us from "elsewhere, unbidden, unexpected and unplanned." The Other tends to "ruin my plans, and if my plans are ruined, that may well be a sign that something is morally binding upon me."[17]

---

[17] Judith Butler, *Precarious Life: The Powers of Mourning and Violence* (New York: Verso, 2004), 130.

Emmanuel Levinas introduced the notion of the "face" to explain how the suffering other makes a moral claim upon us:

> The approach to the face is the most basic mode of respon-
> sibility. . . . The face is not in front of me but above me *(en
> face de moi)*; it is the other before death, looking through and
> exposing death. Secondly, the face is the other who asks me
> not to let him die alone, as if to do so were to become an
> accomplice in his death. Thus the face says to me: you shall
> not kill. In the relation to the face I am exposed as a usurper
> of the place of the other. The celebrated "right to existence"
> . . . is challenged by the relation to the face. Accordingly,
> my duty to respond to the other suspends my natural right
> to self-survival, *le droit vitale*. My ethical relation of love for
> the other stems from the fact that the self cannot survive by
> itself alone, cannot find meaning within its own being-in-the
> world. . . . To expose myself to the vulnerability of the face
> is to put my ontological right to existence into question. In
> ethics, the other's right to exist has primacy over my own,
> a primacy epitomized in the ethical edict: you shall not kill,
> you shall not jeopardize the life of the other.[18]

Levinas makes it clear that

> face . . . is not exclusively the face of man. In Vasily Grossman's
> *Life and Fate* (Part Three, Chapter 23), there is mention of a
> visit to the Lubianka in Moscow by the families or wives or
> relatives of political prisoners, to get news of them. A line
> is formed in front of the windows, in which they can only

---

[18] Emmanuel Levinas and Richard Kearney, "Dialogue with Emmanuel Levinas," in *Face to Face with Levinas* (Albany: SUNY Press, 1986), 23–24, as cited in
Judith Butler, *Precarious Life*, 131–32.

see each other's backs. A woman waits for her turn: "Never had she thought the human back could be so expressive and transmit states of mind so penetratingly. The people who approached the window had a special way of stretching the neck and back; the raised shoulders had shoulder-blades tensed as if by springs, and they seemed to shout, to cry, to sob." Face as the extreme precariousness of the other. Peace as awakening to the precariousness of the other.[19]

The power of the face to make a moral claim upon us is relative to the proximity of the suffering other. The nearness of the suffering other prohibits, or at least makes harder, our inclination to keep suffering at a distance by making abstractions like "the suffering" or constructing objectifying categories such as "the homeless." When suffering others are abstracted and totalized, that is, removed from their place of standing before and over us in all their particularity and precariousness, we are more likely to be complacent about their suffering and complicit in aiding and abetting it. Our complacency and complicity are aided and abetted by a culture that works overtime to keep suffering others out of sight. City planners and councils regularly ponder how to hide the homeless in their midst. Peace, as Levinas suggests, begins with resituating the suffering other near, before, and over us.

A 1972 *Time* magazine front-page photo of a Vietnamese girl running down a road naked after a napalm attack helped turn the tide against the Vietnam War. The photo exposed the violence of our nation's flippant objectification of the "enemy" as "gook." The June 14, 2018, *New York Times* front-page photo of a wailing two-year-old child about to be separated from his Honduran mother at the southern border of the United States aroused widespread

---

[19] Emmanuel Levinas, *Alterity and Transcendence* (London: Athlone Press, 1999), 140.

defiance from what had been a quieter and contained disdain of the Trump administration's border security policies.

## Hospitality

*An act of hospitality can only be poetic.*
—JACQUES DERRIDA, *OF HOSPITALITY*

In Maine, the saying goes, if you follow your dream, you spend a lot of time in the car. This is especially true where I live, in the western foothills. Recently, on the way to a day of offering spiritual direction in a coastal town, I listened to Henryk Gorecki's stirring *Symphony of Sad Songs.* I chose the music as a way to pray the horror of the aforementioned Trump administration's border security policy of separating children from their parents and herding them into vacant Walmart facilities. Words of the second movement: "No, Mother, do not weep, most chaste Queen of Heaven, support me always." The prayer was written on the wall of a Gestapo cell during World War II by an eighteen-year-old woman imprisoned and soon to die.

After the music ended, I switched to the radio, NPR's *Morning Edition*, to hear the headlines. *Top local news:* An employee of Concord Coach Lines, a New England bus company, thinking he was citing company policy, informed ticket holders, before departing the Bangor, Maine, station, that they must be United States citizens to board the bus. *Top national news:* An audio recording of a child in one of the Walmart facilities wailing for his father. *Top international news:* Italy's far-right government announced deportation of the itinerant Roma population.

French philosopher Jacques Derrida, a friend of Emmanuel Levinas, wrote extensively between 1990 and 2004, the year of his death, on hospitality. Derrida's passion for the subject grew out of France's increasingly nationalistic mindset.

Derrida constructed the idea of unconditional hospitality as the ideal from which a nation legislates conditional hospitality:

> Absolute hospitality requires that I open up my home and that I give not only to the foreigner (provided with a family name, with the social status of being a foreigner, etc.) but to the absolute, unknown, anonymous other, and that I *give place* to them, that I let them come, that I let them arrive, and take place in the place I offer them, without asking of them either reciprocity (entering into a pact) or even their names.[20]

Derrida writes that the nature of conditional hospitality includes a certain hostility. That the home is the property of the host imposes on the stranger limitations of space (who is coming?), range of action (dinner is at 6 p.m.), and time (how long do you plan to stay?).[21] I love my times in retreat with wonderfully hospitable brothers. And, of course, both of the monasteries I visit for retreat require answers to these questions. Derrida, in the spirit of Levinas's act of beholding the Other, suggests that truer hospitality is best offered to the guest beyond the threshold of the host. The right of ownership, and the privileges that come with it, make of the host's hospitality a "power over" dynamic.

The atmosphere of hospitality in which we wait with the grieving and aggrieved suggests movement, literally and relationally, from the territory of the beholder to the territory of the beheld. When the post-resurrection Jesus cooked breakfast on the seashore for his

---

[20] Jacques Derrida and Anne Dufourmantelle, *Of Hospitality* (Stanford, CA: Stanford University Press, 2000), 25.

[21] Gerasimos Kakoliris, "Jacques Derrida on the Ethics of Hospitality," in *The Ethics of Subjectivity: Perspectives since the Dawn of Modernity*, ed. Elvis Imafidon (London: Palgrave McMillan, 2015), 148–49.

bereaved disciples, who were fishermen, he prepared fish on *their* beach, his fish *and* their fish.[22]

When building the Hospice at Mission Hill, we collaborated with the finest interior designers in the northeastern United States to create spaces that were extravagantly welcoming—prints of Robert Mapplethorpe photographs, one ceiling painted as clouds, another as a trellis entwined with grape vines. Our guests mostly were unimpressed. We had prepared deathbeds at the Ritz. They desired deathbeds that reflected the spirit and tastes of the homes they had to leave.

With hands carrying carefully prepared recipes of compassion, we are apt to trip over the rug of our cultural biases and power advantage, spilling our goodwill in the laps of our guests. Godly hospitality is a moveable feast, one that literally and figuratively moves from our hearths to the hearths of our neighbors. Hospitality that empowers those dislocated by loss and trauma decenters the host and centers the guest. As decentered hosts we will feel awkward and disempowered as the ones interpreted rather than the ones interpreting, as those beheld in uncomfortable ways by the beneficiaries of our regard. Our disorientation possibly is the strongest connection we have to the disoriented ones to whom we attend. We become more like than unlike them. The distance between witness and testifier closes. Mutuality is established.

When we imagine the impossibility, the contradiction, of hospitality as generally understood and practiced, we are better equipped and inspired to reposition ourselves with respect to the stranger, the other: "'Come to the step of the other,' to the step of Elijah at our door, to the step of the absolute surprise, so that the other will not

---

[22] Robert J. Schreiter, *The Ministry of Reconciliation: Spiritualities and Strategies* (Maryknoll, NY: Orbis Books, 1998), 89.

be the mirror image of my 'psyche.' If anything, it is I who will be invented by the other."[23]

## Reiteration

When we stay in a learning position about the stories people tell about their lives, particularly stories about sorrow, suffering, and trauma, new perspectives and possibilities emerge. Two conditions apply: (1) the listeners resist the temptation to tamper with the stories, and (2) the listeners create space for the stories to be told again and again, and then again. When these conditions are met, the testifiers may hear themselves again as if for the first time.

Harlene Anderson remarks that fiction sometimes better captures what she tries to convey. See, for example, the following words of Smilla, protagonist in Peter Hoeg's *Smilla's Sense of Snow*:

> Very few people know how to listen. Their haste pulls them out of the conversation, or they try internally to improve the situation, or they're preparing what their entrance will be when you shut up and it's their turn to step on stage. . . . It's different with the man standing in front of me. When I talk he listens without distraction to what I say, and only to what I say.[24]

Anderson writes that "change emerges in and through the re-descriptions that result from telling and retelling of familiar stories. In the telling and retelling not only do new stories emerge, but a person changes in relationship to them: the narrating self is

---

[23] John Caputo, *The Prayers and Tears of Jacques Derrida: Religion without Religion* (Bloomington: Indiana University Press, 1997), 73.

[24] Peter Hoeg, *Smilla's Sense of Snow* (McHenry, IL: Delta Publishing Company, 1993), 44–45.

changed."[25] There is no telling how often stories of sorrow, suffering, and tragedy need repeating in order for a new perspective, a glimpse of meaning, an unforeseen path, a previously unimaginable forgiveness, a once-closed future to open. What we do know is that the arc of lament is long and bends toward liberation. We make our way moment to moment. Lament is a process we do not complete in this life. That we continue the process grounds us in emancipatory community now.

## Marking Absence

*Even if the killer tells you that your father's bones are in a toilet, you go to those pits and pull them out.*

—TERRY TEMPEST WILLIAMS,
*FINDING BEAUTY IN A BROKEN WORLD*

The morning after the execution of Jesus, women went to the tomb to anoint his body. Jesus was not there. Mary Magdalene's anxious cry is a collect over their desperation: "They have taken away my Lord and I do not know where they have laid him" (Jn 20:13).

Public lament begins with companions walking toward an empty tomb, a labyrinth circling to a center of absence, where together we stand and cry for our loved ones and ourselves. As a Chilean woman said: "Every time I see a madman or a hobo in the street, I think it may be my husband, or that he might be somewhere in a similar situation."[26] The one request of a woman who lost a son to apartheid was that South Africa provide a tombstone for a body never found. At a commemoration event at Bates College in April

---

[25] Harlene Anderson, *Conversation, Language, and Possibilities: A Postmodern Approach to Therapy* (New York: Basic Books, 1997), 109.

[26] Schreiter, *The Ministry of Reconciliation*, 33.

2009, marking the fifteenth anniversary of the 1994 genocide of the Tutsis in Rwanda, Carine Gakuba, a survivor, said that she returned to Rwanda to confront the man who murdered her father. She shared that her principal desire in the confrontation was to find out where her father was killed so that she could visit the place. Her desire to mark the absence was much stronger than her need for a word, whatever word, from her father's killer. A survivor of child sexual abuse prays for clearer memories of her body's violation to return, as painful as they may be, so that she will have a place from which to orient her horror.

Bryan Stevenson, referenced in the previous chapter, is executive director of the Equal Justice Initiative in Montgomery, Alabama. One of the initiative's projects is a ritual of marking the places where blacks were lynched. He travels to lynching sites. He stands with the survivors of the murdered relatives on the ground where they were hung, burned, shot, disembodied, from which they were dragged through black neighborhoods to scare blacks into submission. Soil from the site is gathered by the survivors. Each jar of soil, along with descriptions of the murdered men, women, or children will be placed in a museum now under construction.

As mentioned earlier, I spent eight years among people dying from AIDS during the first wave of the pandemic. Those who died were young and, for the most part, healthy prior to the onset of the disease. One of the most haunting dimensions of their dying was the horrific wasting and disfigurement of their bodies. I remember the passion with which we created their panels for the national AIDS quilt displayed in Washington, DC. We sought to recapture the profiles of their once-sufficient and embodied lives.

Our relation to those who have died or disappeared does not end—it changes. Yet change demands a touchstone from which to depart:

> The children entered the room where Steve's body lay. They touched his feet; they touched his arms and felt them as

cold. They moved closer and lovingly rubbed his forehead. Respectful. Curious. And then, one by one they began to cry. One person said, "Steve was my best friend." Another said, "I miss him." Within minutes, the children were sitting on the bed alongside his body telling stories about their uncle. Fear was transformed into comfort, curiosity melted into love, and the silence was no longer uncomfortable.[27]

Marking death and disappearance in concrete and material ways begins the restorative journey. Most liturgies of the church, especially those that survive the ages, recollect salvation history's experiences of trauma, absence, and loss, with baptism and Eucharist chief among them. We have our aforementioned salvation history of "dangerous memories" that deconstruct the too-sufficient church's rituals of forgetting the cross. We have the voices of present victims, who, when heard to voice, can collaborate with the stewards of ritual and liturgy to mark the tombstones of their sorrow and anguish. As I write now, I wish that my daughter's recent miscarriage could have been ritualized by my son-in-law's and her church community. I do know that this is a practice in some churches. As we gather around victims and their co-created tombstones, their memories become the community's memory. The community's memory is threatening to the stasis that preserves the dominance of temple and town.

## The Spirit of Curiosity

I sometimes approach Jesus's big questions in a manner different from the more conventional angle of teachable moments.[28]

---

[27] Terry Tempest Williams, *Finding Beauty in a Broken World* (New York: Pantheon Books, 2008), 207.

[28] Ideas about the curious Jesus germinated in Blaine-Wallace, "Post Christian Pastoral Care."

"But who do you say that I am?" (Lk 9:20). Approaching Jesus's big questions as interrogation of our faith privileges belief over discipleship. Belief in Jesus is convenient for a culture that would be turned inside out if the church acted like Jesus. I like to pray Jesus's big questions as more strategic than rhetorical. Jesus as the zealous servant and disquieted leader of an emancipatory movement needed to ask certain questions in the service of reconciling the estranged, restoring the lost, liberating the captive. I imagine Jesus asking questions on the fly in the service of the moment for the sake of the movement.

"But who do you say that I am?" Other than the doctrinal construction of Jesus as God incarnate, with a pedagogy of waiting for the right answer from his followers, might Jesus also be one new companion wondering about how he and his other new companions might go on together?

"Do you want to be made well?" (Jn 5:6). Do you want to be healed? Are you kidding? Thirty-eight years on a filthy mat waiting for someone to put you in a sacred pool when the angel disturbs the water. Could it be that Jesus needed some information?

He asks the man possessed by many demons, "What is your name?" (Lk 8:30). I like to think of Jesus trying to make friends with one scared, scary, and lonely guy in addition to chasing some pigs over a cliff on the man's behalf (Lk 8:32–33).

Anyway, I benefit from imagining Jesus as insatiably nosy and unapologetically green as he ministered to and with unfamiliar people in uncertain times. I find the icon of Jesus as the near-to-the-ground inquirer of neighbor to be inspiring and empowering as I make my way among and for those I am called to serve.

Curiosity—expressed by questions that matter at the moment, relate to the issue at hand, not offered to test an assumption, and aim toward imagined but not overdetermined emancipation—is the cornerstone upon which the rudiments of lament are built. I sense when witnesses receive my testimony in a quieter, respectful, attentive manner, *and*, from the edge of their seat. Theirs is a still-ness that inquisitively leans into my multidimensional utterances—words, silences, sighs, diverted glances, twiddling thumbs, blushes, tears, and other utterances of which I am unaware. Their stance of waiting, not until but always, opens space for me to traverse unset-tling, unfamiliar territory in a direction that is unclear but promis-ing. We are on new ground. Each of us will leave the encounter different from who we were when we began the conversation.

Here is the prayer I offer in the silence before I, as a witness, hear another's testimony:

> May I not ask questions I think I know the an-
> swer to.
> May I ask only ask questions that emanate from
> my neighbor's utterances.
> May I not offer words when I have none to
> give.
> Help me distrust hunches.
> Help me accompany, not deliver. Amen.

In the next chapter we learn a conversational method that offers us a good chance, a hearty way, to integrate the seven foundational elements discussed above into lament-oriented communities and relations. While we may not feel comfortable using the method in a rote way, or have the contexts to implement it, the values and commitments upon which it is based vivify conversational partner-ships that matter.

# 7

# The Shadow of Paradise

*Even though I walk through the valley of the*
*shadow of death,*
*I fear no evil, for You are with me;*
*Your rod and Your staff, they comfort me.*
—Psalm 23:4, NASB

A really hard winter has passed. The snow is almost gone. Buds are forming on the trees. Red peony stems are starting to break the soil. A new granddaughter has come into our lives. Yet, a fog of disquietedness shrouds these last couple of weeks. Big disconnect. What is going on?

Sometimes the *shadow* of death dims our sense of what particular sorrow, suffering, or trauma has hold of us. We carry an indistinguishable burden that disturbs peace. We do not have means to articulate a prayer about it. The burden is our prayer. We cannot get to lament. Alleluias escape us.

The family Tom Andersen sat with in Chapter 6 had been walking through the valley of the shadow of death. Family and therapist were stuck. What was going on? The wailing of the family, the adolescent grandson's the loudest, echoed off the walls of the therapist's office. Tom accompanied the family to lament mostly by what he did not do. "There is much noise." Words born of a silent listening. "I wonder, if noise could speak, what would noise have to say to us?" A question borne of a gentle curiosity. "Is this too hard to bring to words now? What do you think? Shall we talk or not?" Questions of deep respect and attention. "He leads me beside quiet waters" (Ps 23:2b).

Tom's gift for creating and sustaining lamentational conversations often was offered on a particular relational stage. He developed a method for staging conversations in a manner that distributes expertise and creates new knowledge. The distinction between server and served is relaxed. Wailing is collaboratively transposed into lament. The method is called the *reflecting team*.

Tom developed the reflecting-team process while professor of social psychiatry at the University of Tromsø, Norway. The Royal Norwegian Ministry of Health and Care Services commissioned Tom to develop a program to decrease hospitalization of mental health patients. Between 1978 and 1984, Tom and seven colleagues worked with frontline professionals, mostly family physicians serving far-ranging rural communities.[1]

Tom's team manifested a dimension of Jacques Derrida's idea of "impossible hospitality," which we explored in the last chapter. The team decided not to bring the healthcare professionals to Tromsø for training. Instead, the team went to the "hearths"[2] of the practitioners with whom they consulted. There, as guests, they co-created a process in consultation with the professionals and the persons and families they served. The process evolved through several iterations, each aimed at conversational practices that centered the patients and decentered the professionals for the purpose of co-created knowledge. Moreover, the goal of decreasing hospitalizations was achieved.

---

[1] Tom Andersen, *The Reflecting Team: Dialogues and Dialogues about the Dialogues* (New York and London: W. W. Norton, 1991), 7.

[2] Ibid., 8.

Initially, the reflecting-team process rattled the worldwide family therapy community. The process was attacked as unorthodox at best, dangerous at worst. Over time, the process has become an accepted and increasingly preferred model for family therapy.

I learned the reflecting team process at the Salem Center for Therapy, Training, and Research in Salem, Massachusetts. Tom Andersen consulted with the center. Over time, I have adjusted the reflecting-team process in ways that are more resonant with my sense about and manner of stewarding lamentational conversations. I have integrated certain narrative therapy[3] practices, especially questions we often used in meetings with families at the Salem Center. Most important, I have laicized the process, adjusted it to fit in parish, parish-wide, and nonreligious contexts. I call the method the witnessing process.

In this chapter I introduce the witnessing process and the manner in which I utilized it in two parish settings and one educational setting. At the end of the chapter I provide an outline to use as a handout for guiding the witnessing process. My intention is that at the end of the chapter, you, the reader, will have enough information to give it a try. I know from experience that the process can at times be scary and tempt conveners to abandon it in the middle of conversations that matter. I have learned, the hard way, that if I trust the process, take deep breaths, and not steer from it at delicate and agonal moments, the vast majority of the time all will be well.

## Conversation 1:
## Quieting Assumptions and Building Relational Knowledge

After retiring from Bates College, I served a parish in rural Maine. The parish comprises approximately twenty-five people. When I

---

[3] For an introduction to narrative therapy, see https://dulwichcentre.com.au/. The Dulwich Centre in Adelaide, Australia, is the birthplace of narrative therapy.

arrived, I imagined that members of the family-size parish knew one another well, especially the seven to ten people who have kept the doors open for the last decade or so.

As I came to know them, I rediscovered what I know but am quick to forget: our knowledge of people is negatively affected by assumptions that creep into relations through interactions that produce a sense of familiarity. Our narratives about the people with whom we are in ongoing relation sometimes size up and objectify the other in ways that hinder and damage the relational space between us. There were a lot of less than life-giving narratives about members floating around the parish. We had work to do.

The work was about expanding the heart of community to a size that would enable the parishioners to go on together in less destructive and unsettling ways. By that I do not mean a way to make parishioners nicer, though that is often a benefit for a while. The work is about creating a "front porch" for people to hang out on in a particular way; a space for people to remain in a learning position, respectfully attentive and curious; a space from which new possibilities and ways of going on together can emerge.

During the first Lenten season at the parish I facilitated a series titled "Roads to Saint Simeon."[4] Each Sunday, after worship, for five Sundays, a person shared the story of how he or she came to be a part of the Saint Simeon community. The story was less about the history of each person's journey to the parish, and more an offering of his or her spiritual journey from earliest memory to the present.

I selected presenters who represented the broad spectrum of spiritualities represented in the parish.[5] Jerry, about seventy years old, who identifies as agnostic, has attended the church for about thirty years. He comes for the community he experiences at Saint Simeon. He hosts a monthly coffeehouse in the church basement;

---

[4] Saint Simeon is a pseudonym.
[5] The following names are pseudonyms.

it has become a staple event over the years in the wider community. John, also around seventy years old, a high school math teacher, is senior warden of the vestry, the elected body of the parish, and has been a member of the church for about fifteen years. For John, the parish represents a place to ground his faith, a faith shaped by a difficult childhood. Agnes, about ninety years old, is a matriarch of the parish. She is a devout Christian of a more biblically grounded, conservative tradition. Mary, about seventy-five years old, is a retired nurse and spouse of a retired minister. She has strong faith, which provides her with a clear sense of self, neighbor, and God. She is a grounding presence in the parish. Teresa, about sixty years old, is a newer member of the parish. She is a retired actor who acted professionally in New York City and taught theater in a university before settling in Maine. Theresa's father taught at a mainline Christian boarding school. She grew up on the campus, where she regularly attended worship. Theresa came to Saint Simeon because she wanted to return to church after several decades away.

Each week, the hour-long process began with a few minutes of prayerful silence. I then interviewed one of the five storytellers for about twelve minutes. We started the conversation wherever the interviewee desired. I did little prior coaching in terms of what the interviewee was to offer, and I had little to say as interviewer. I gingerly followed my curiosity and mentioned a few words that caught my attention. I resisted the temptations that often visit interviewers—having an agenda and trying to "get at" the meaning or purpose of what the interviewee shares.

After the initial interview a witnessing team of three to five people from the audience shared among themselves their experience of the interview. The team sat together, several feet from the interviewee and me. The team members reflected among themselves for about twelve minutes. They were instructed not to speak from an analyzing, critiquing, advising position. When they did, I gently brought them back to a reflecting position.

I provided several questions as guidelines for the witnessing team to refer to as a way to shape their conversation. Where were you moved, touched by what you heard? What is important to the storyteller in terms of values, commitments, desires? How is the storyteller's experience similar to yours; that is, where is the empathic connection? What new knowledge did you acquire by witnessing the storyteller's offering, and more specifically, how are you different having experienced the testimony? What symbol, metaphor, song, piece of art, and so on, sums up your experience as a witness; that is, what can you hold on to as a way to remember what you experienced? Finally, what questions would you have liked the interviewer to ask the storyteller; in other words, what are you curious about?

Next, the week's storyteller—Jerry, for example—had about five minutes to reflect on the witnessing team's offerings. Where was he moved? What did he hear about himself that gave him a different, new, forgotten sense of self? What would he like to explore, how would he like to continue the conversation with the witnessing team? The opportunity to silently witness others' experience of our testimonies is a rare gift.

Then came the heart of the conversation. All those in attendance, especially those who had yet to speak because they were not on the witnessing team, about twelve people, were invited to converse for about thirty minutes about what we all had experienced. What's important? What are we learning about our life together? What might we do with what we have learned?

Prior to the beginning of this hour-long process, I shared a few thoughts for the attendees to consider as the process unfolded. The interviewee was not the primary focus of the process. Rather, the interviewee's offering was "starter dough" for a wider conversation about matters that matter. If some attendees did not put words to their reflections, that did not mean they were not participating and contributing to the experience. I talked about our inner (silent) and outer (vocal) voices. Each participant brings two voices to the conversation. Seventeen participants account for thirty-four voices. Inner voices were active whether they spoke or not. I reminded participants to keep inner and outer offerings in a reflective rather than critiquing, analyzing, advising spirit.

After each of the five sessions the atmosphere was deeply convivial. Sometimes tears were shared. Experiences were offered that brought the audience to prayerful silence. There were lighter, laughter-filled moments. God had disappeared into the lamentational choir and arose, at times, as a palpable and contagious conviviality and joy. Attendees had come to a place, mentioned in Chapter 4, of *seeing* rather than *looking at* one another. Attendees left church changed.

The half-life of resurrection peace is not as long as we imagine, however. During the latter part of my ministry at Saint Simeon's, I rested on the laurels of these earlier "roads to Saint Simeon." I failed to create more and ongoing witnessing processes adjusted to meet particular situations and occasions of assumptive behaviors, experiences where we were looking at rather than seeing one another. The witnessing process is more than a parish event now and again. It is foundational to lament as ecclesiology. My experience suggests that witnessing processes, of one iteration or another, are best offered at least quarterly. I will speak about other iterations later in the chapter.

## Lamentational Foundations of the Witnessing Process

There are values and commitments underlying the witnessing process that are in the service of lamentational ecclesiology. The witnessing process invites participants into a shared God event, a trinitarian dance in which one and all participate. The witnessing process enables conversational partners to stay in a respectful, attentive position. Such sturdiness stewards a curiosity that arouses the inner and outer voices of all participants, a collection of co-created, mutual, nonhierarchical utterances.

The reverential nature of the witnessing process creates safer space for participants to bring inner voices to the outer conversation. Sorrow, suffering, and trauma do not need to be teased out. When we reflect on the history of our lived experience, the brokenness of our lives emerges in and through the conversation to the degree that the conversation remains reflective, respectfully curious, and void of interpretation and advice. Because the witnessing process awakens more regions of the heart, the conversational partnership helps move congregations through the wailing-lament-solidarity-joy-justice trajectory expressive of salvation history. The congregation engages in the kind of psalmic language explored in Chapters 1 and 2.

### Dynamics of the Witnessing Process

The witnessing process is means and end. The conversation is the cure. The witnessing process is an event of conversation for conversation's sake. Witnessing conversations liberate in ways not imagined nor predetermined. Witnessing conversations open relational space from which possibilities and direction emerge and bless life together. The challenge is to keep the conversations going, to make time and space for them, and to imagine situations that would benefit from them. Witnessing conversations are a way to go on together, to keep going on together.

The format of the witnessing process helps prevent conversational partners from falling back into the "power over" dynamic of pastor/parishioner, leader/member, old member/newcomer. The witnessing process is "a political act whose function is to distribute power among all the different voices in the discourse, dominant and nondominant."[6]

Pastors and parishioners, mirroring our society, move along a too linear path: season to season, meeting to meeting, dollar to dollar, one pastoral and congregational crisis to another. We are dutiful, "building logging roads, putting up bridges, and various other engineering projects" to make a difference for the good and to stay sufficiently solvent.[7] The witnessing process allows the congregation to slow down community to a pace that invites attention to the moment. Each participant jumps into the pool of tears with others. And, most often, to the delight of all.

## Contexts for the Witnessing Process

I have used the witnessing process over many years in several contexts and for different purposes—for family and couples counseling, church leadership retreats, mediating congregational differences and conflicts, and as pedagogy for adult education. The model adjusts well to the matter at hand—spiritual journey, relational challenges, engaging sensitive matters and difficult conversations, clarifying and imagining congregational strategy and mission, and staging diocesan plenary conversations.

## The Witnessing Process Challenges the Convener

Conveners of the witnessing process manage two challenges in their stewardship of the process. First, they ensure that the initial testifier/

---

[6] James Griffith and Melissa Griffith, *The Body Speaks: Therapeutic Dialogues for Mind-Body Problems* (New York: Basic Books, 1994), 166.

[7] Lynn Hoffman, "The Art of Witness: A New Bright Edge," in *Collaborative Therapy: Relationships and Conversations That Make a Difference,* ed. H. Anderson and D. Gehart (New York: Routledge, 2007), 66.

interviewee is empowered by an interviewer/witness who stays in a curious position and does not guide the conversation. Often witnesses/interviewers are tempted to probe for meaning, "get at" something, which takes the interview more in the direction of the interviewer and away from the testifier's/interviewee's "confession" of life-the-way-it-really-is. Second, the convener ensures that the witnessing team and wider audience stay in a reflecting position that precludes analysis-critique-advice. When reflection and curiosity are abandoned for the sake of getting our two cents in, we move from conversation about life-the-way-it-really-is to life-the-way-it-might-be. When the reflecting spirit is compromised, the trajectory of wailing-lament-solidarity-joy-justice is thwarted. The handout "Witnessing Process Outline," which I give to the witness/interviewee and the witnessing team, helps meet these challenges; it is presented at the end of the chapter.

## Conversation 2:
## Strengthening Congregational Relations

A letter from God to Margaret, an incest survivor:

Dear Margaret,

I know you find it difficult to fit into your womanhood; but I want you to know how proud I am of you and that I am with you on this journey as are your mother and grandmother. We walk with you. We were with you as you marched in that first march in Bangor to bring awareness to the community about abuse. We were with you when the man from a window emptied his beer and threw an egg on your head. You kept on walking. Your tear is my tear. You have helped many women be able to tell their story as you started the first incest-awareness days in the area. You may not have given birth biologically, but you have birthed something equally wonderful—a new generation of women without abuse. You are the beacon of the lighthouse you see. You broke the cycle by your willingness to publicly tell your story. You spoke of the unspoken. I know you feel guilty sometimes because you were not able to protect your sister Betty, but it wasn't your fault. You did not know. I know that it cost you when Mark was abusing women that you sent to him for pastoral care. It hurt you deeply. It hurt me too. I know you continue to struggle with trust issues, especially with bishops. You also continue to struggle with body image and being female. You have healed much from your incest. I can walk this part of your journey with trusting the church. You have a right to be angry. You have a right to walk away. I know your pain of feeling betrayed by someone and something you loved. You love deeply. I know you went away from me last spring and chose not to do your morning meditations. This is your first retreat in a long time. I am glad you are back.

The letter emerged at a parish retreat I designed and led utilizing the witnessing process. Prior to the retreat I had a conversation with the parish priest, Rick, a colleague and friend. He came to the farm. We walked the meandering trail mentioned in Chapter 5. Along the way we imagined outcomes of the retreat. I created a scenario. "Rick, the retreat has just ended. You overhear two parishioners talking on the way to their cars. One says to the other, 'That was exactly what I hoped for, perfect retreat!' What are they so excited about?" Rick responded, "Their bonds with one another and with God have been strengthened. And not just by good conversation. Art. I want us to make art together." The title of the retreat was the same as the title of this book: *When Tears Sing: The Art of Lament in Christian Community.*

The retreat was scheduled for Saturday lunch through Sunday lunch. The setting was beautiful, a couple of oceanfront, adjoining

homes on Mount Desert Island. Rick secured a supply priest for
Sunday worship back home for those who could not make the
retreat. Sessions were scheduled between great meals and creative
liturgies for Noonday Prayer, Evening Prayer, Compline, Morning
Prayer, and Eucharist.

*Session One* (Saturday afternoon): I asked the participants to
remember a particular tear they had shed over the course of their
lives. One that would be hard to forget. Imagine the tear—sad,
joyful, searing (the kind that stings the eyes), big and full (as in
overwhelmed by an emotion or experience). I asked them to take
a walk or have a seat with their tear. Pray questions about the tear.
What was the occasion for the tear? Imagine the tear as a room.
Who and what were in the room of the tear? Take about thirty
minutes with your tear. When we gather back together, we'll make
art of our tears—a drawing, poem, letter, song, rap, whatever. Rick
brought lots of art materials. I asked participants to pair off and
share their "tear-art" to the degree that they felt safe doing so. After
about thirty minutes we gathered back together. Each pair shared
what they had learned about their partner through the offering of
their tears.

*Session Two* (Saturday evening): I asked for a volunteer, a person
who might benefit from further conversation with the group about
his or her tear. I shared that we would use the witnessing process
for the conversation. I would interview the person about the tear.
A witnessing team of three to five people would then reflect on
our interview using particular questions to guide the conversation.
Where were you moved? What's important to this person? How
was this person's tear more like than different from other tears (the
empathic question)? What did you learn from the interview that
you will carry home with you? What would you have liked the
interviewer to ask about the tear during the initial interview, that
is, what are you curious about? What symbol, song, or visual art
captures your experience of the initial interview? The interviewee

would then have a chance to reflect on the witnessing team's reflection before we opened the floor for all to add their voices to the conversation. I shared that the person offering his or her tear in the initial interview would not be the subject of the wider conversation. Rather, that initial offering was a catalyst for the wider conversation about the effects of shared tears in parish life. I talked about the relational silence each of us brings to the conversation, our inner voice. I shared that some will keep reflections to themselves, others offer them to the community. I remarked that silence is an active presence in and for community.

A lamentational chorus ensued, the spirit of which spilled over into Compline and post-Compline conversation.

*Session Three* (Sunday morning after Morning Prayer): I asked participants to bring their tear-art with them to the Sunday morning session. I asked them to think of the one person who would really "get" their tear. Who would best understand and desire to hear about the tear? Whose words about the tear would matter most? With whom would they feel most safe sharing their tear? I asked them to take these persons on a thirty-minute walk with them and their tear, and then find a quiet place to transcribe a letter to them from their companion. Questions arose. Do you mean write a letter to the companion or from the companion? From the companion. Really? How can we know what our companion would write? Don't overthink it. Simply let your hand have its way. Simply record your companion's words. See what happens.

When we gathered back together, I did not ask the participants to pair off. I trusted that to do so may not feel safe, that the letter might be too precious to share at the moment. Rather, I invited participants to share what the experience was like, what they received, learned, treasured from the correspondence. I asked what they might share in a return letter.

After a break I asked for a volunteer who felt that he or she might benefit from and feel safe offering the letter for another witnessing process. The process mirrored the form of the previous evening's witnessing process. The lamentational chorus evoked by the witnessing process spilled over and into the closing Eucharist.

## Conversation 3:
## The Diversity Workshop

During my years at Bates College, the Bates Office Professionals Network (BOPN) offered a relational space for administrative assistants, a space for support and a means to address concerns. Often they stood with and for one another as victims of classism. They were oppressed by attitudes and behaviors, policies, and practices that consigned them to the margins of campus discourses.

The BOPN leadership was asked by the Office of Affirmative Action and Diversity Projects to offer a workshop for BOPN members on diversity. I was consulted as one who has worked on diversity issues from a narrative orientation. We designed a daylong experience during which narratives of marginalization were offered in a safe, confidential space.

The leadership team worked hard to recruit participants. Members of BOPN did not jump at the prospect of a workshop on diversity. They were weary of what felt like the college's concern about everybody's experience of discrimination but theirs. Also, they were afraid that there would be repercussions if they spoke their minds. The leadership team assured BOPN members that the day would be more than, and different from, a complaint session, and that the narratives that unfolded would not be the property of anyone but themselves. When the director of human resources stood behind the event, some of the fear abated.

The day began with the director of human resources welcoming the participants and sharing a story about an experience where he felt marginalized because of his lower status on the organizational chart. I then spent about thirty minutes talking about the power of stories and the manner in which we would share them at the workshop. After my presentation, we started the five-step process.

*Step One* (table experience): The participants remained in their seats at their assigned tables. In the middle of each table was a childhood toy. The participants shared stories related to the toy.

*Step Two* (plenary experience): We used the witnessing process. A member of the leadership team was interviewed about her experience growing up as a non-English speaking French Canadian in Lewiston (Maine). I asked for volunteers for the witnessing team. People were slow to volunteer. After a few minutes we had three volunteers, enough to proceed. During the witnessing process vibrant conversation ensued. French Canadians in Maine, for most of the twentieth century, were targets of intense discrimination. Maine, in fact, in the early twentieth century, had the nation's largest per capita membership in the Ku Klux Klan.

*Step Three* (table experience): A large pencil eraser was placed on each table. Participants were invited to share stories of feeling or being "erased" at Bates. A new courage and sense of mission as well as a spirit of solidarity around suffering emerged.

*Step Four* (plenary experience): Again, we used the witnessing process. This time, participants more quickly volunteered to be on the witnessing team. The testifier/interviewee was interviewed not by me but by another participant. The testifier/interviewee shared a momentous experience of being erased at Bates and her struggle and success at overcoming the erasure. The interviewee concluded by standing up and singing, "All I Want Is a Room Somewhere." She received a standing ovation.

*Step Five* (plenary experience): The day concluded with an evaluation process designed as an open dialogue. The major outcome of the open dialogue was that the energy of the day should not be lost and that future conversations should be expanded to include the wider college community.

The spirit of the day did spill over into the wider community. The president of the college asked for the leadership team to write up a report, which she presented at the next meeting of the trustees. Three new initiatives emerged from the workshop: a summer retreat, a presentation at the annual Martin Luther King Jr. Memorial Day Workshop, and a presentation during Staff Development Week at the end of the academic year.

About thirty people attended the summer retreat (the first initiative). Before the retreat participants read *Warriors Don't Cry: A Searing Memoir of the Battle to Integrate Little Rock's Central High School* by Melba Pattillo Beals, one of the nine students selected by the NAACP to integrate the high school.

Participants in the original workshop experienced a solidarity around their oppression that inspired them to learn about the oppression of others. Participants were eager to learn more about racial oppression and to participate in the wider diversity initiative at Bates and in the wider Lewiston community, which, at the time, was embroiled in conflict over the large influx of Somali refugees.

The second initiative was a presentation on *Warriors Don't Cry* at the 2008 annual Martin Luther King Jr. Memorial Day Workshop at Bates, a widely acclaimed and respected event, a highlight of the academic calendar at Bates. The third initiative was a diversity workshop at the first annual staff development week. "Graduates" of the initial BOPN workshop led the workshop. In the evaluations this workshop received the highest score.

## The Shadow of Paradise

I have brought my affairs home to God, . . .
If I should live yet longer here . . .
I shall not struggle against it.

—BACH, CANTATA 106

These words are from Bach's Cantata 106, his funeral cantata, which begins with the words, "God's time is the best of times; for living or dying," arguably one of Bach's more intimate cantatas.[8] The chorus and orchestration are spare, and the foundational instruments are two recorders. The recorders open the cantata with a unison duet that is hauntingly beautiful. After the duet the recorders delightfully and sublimely weave through the cantata.

Before a performance of the cantata by the Netherlands Bach Society on November 8, 2018, conducted by Jos van Veldhoven, the principal recorder player, Heiko ter Schegget, reflected on Bach's use of recorders for the cantata. He said that Bach chose the hardest instrument to play in unison and for finding perfect pitch. What was Bach up to? The beauty of the recorder is its wonderfully simple, almost raspy sound that resides in the shadow of perfect pitch. Shadow. I like to imagine that Bach opened Cantata 106 with recorders to signify life this side of heaven, life in the shadow of death.

The only time the recorder is silenced in the cantata is during the bass aria/alto chorale, the words of which are "Today you will be with Me in Paradise" (Lk 23:43). The recorder player remarked, "The only time I can't play is in paradise!"[9]

When we find and make community for shared tears, our walk in the shadow of death becomes an experience that brings us into the shadow of the eternal. Through the blur of shared sorrow, suffering, and trauma, we faintly glimpse God (1 Cor 13:12). Our desire for heaven is quickened.

Consider these words from Irene's aria, from Händel's oratorio *Theodora*, shortly after the noblewoman Theodora's conversion to the Christian faith, for which she was martyred:

---

[8] Translations are from the website of Emmanuel Music. Emmanuel Music provides notes for and translations of all the Bach cantatas.

[9] Netherlands Bach Society, "Van der Velden, Van Veldhoven and Ter Schegget on Bach Cantata BWV 106" (November 8, 2018), available on YouTube.

> As with rosy steps the morn,
> Advancing, drives the shades of night,
> So from virtuous toils well-borne,
> Raise Thou our hopes of endless light.
> Triumphant saviour, Lord of day,
> Thou art the life, the light, the way![10]

I find that the witnessing process is one way for parishes to enhance the possibility of experiencing the shadow of death's transposition to the shadow of paradise.

On the following page is the handout I distribute to the interviewee and witnessing team prior to the witnessing process.

---

[10] Georg Friedrich Händel, *Theodora,* scene 4. The libretto is available at opera.stanford.edu/iu/libretti/theodora.htm.

# THE WITNESSING PROCESS HANDOUT

The witnessing process establishes a conversation that involves all attendees and creates a greater possibility for thickening relation and generating new knowledge.

1.  The interview will last about twelve to fifteen minutes, an organic, unrehearsed conversation. The interviewer practices "near experience" listening, which attends to the words actually spoken, not what the interviewer "heard." Interpretation of what the interviewee said—for example, "I heard you saying . . ."—is *not* a road to go down.

2.  After the interview the witnessing team members reflect among themselves about the interview they have witnessed. The witnessing team conversation also is about twelve to fifteen minutes. The reflections among the team members are not to move along the lines of critique or advice. Rather, the witnessing team conversation is loosely framed by the following questions:

    *   While you were listening to the conversation between the interviewee and the interviewer, what did you hear that you were most drawn to? Words? Phrases? Images? Ideas?
    *   As you listened, what did the conversation suggest to you about what might be important to this person? Values? Commitments? Priorities? Desires? Hopes?
    *   What is it about your own experience that created a resonance, a bond, a connection with what the interviewee shared? Where did you notice that you felt a difference, a variation, another idea or additional idea in regard to what you heard?
    *   Having listened to the conversation, what new ideas, discoveries, knowledge have you acquired, which you may not have received without hearing this

conversation? How will you leave this conversation different from how you came to it?

- What are you curious about? What do you want to know more about? What questions do you wish the interviewer had asked the interviewee?
- Is there a symbol, a metaphor that captures your experience of the conversation, something that enables you to remember and continue to reflect on the experience?

3.  After the witnessing team conversation, the interviewee will have about five minutes to share his or her reflections on the witnessing team conversation.

4.  Most important, the conversation is opened to the audience so that the audience's reflections carry on and enrich the conversation. The audience conversation is the principal voice of the conversation.

*Important to note:*

1.  The reflections of the witnessing team and audience are not about the interviewee's story. Rather, the initial interview is "starter dough" for an audience-wide conversation about the theme of the gathering. That being said, a great way to prepare for participation on the witnessing team is to be mindful, prior to the event, of your own personal experiences and perspectives related to the theme.

2.  Silence is golden! Silence is not the withholding of words. Silence is the reflecting spirit that is alive in and between all present. It is a very active voice. Some will put words to their inner voices and offer them to the group. Others will not. That voices are not put to words does not mean a lack of participation in the process.

# 8

# Stubborn Melancholy

## *Lessons from Emmanuel Church*

Lament is an ecclesiology of the shadows. Tears sing at the still point at which turn the shadows of death and paradise. Wailing dissolves into lament.

Under the ambient light of empire, the church stays up all night and, exhausted, falls asleep just shy of dawn. The earliest morning hues of shared sorrow, suffering, and trauma too often pass us by. We are bereft of the awe and amazement that blesses, awakens, and restores. Lament wails.

In Händel's oratorio *Theodora*, just after Theodora's friend Irene has completed the exquisite aria, "As with rosy steps the morn," the soldiers of fourth-century Antioch, then a Roman province of Syria, come to arrest noblewoman Theodora for her conversion to the Christian faith. The soldiers startle the gathering of Christians, which has just celebrated Theodora's conversion. The soldiers' haste is related to a decree of Valens, the Roman governor of Antioch. In honor of Emperor Diocletian's birthday, all citizens of Antioch must offer sacrifice to Venus, goddess of love, and Flora, a fertility goddess of springtime. Those who refuse risk death. In an aria, Septimius, Valens's right-hand man, in an ironically pleading tone, mocks the gathering's faith:

Dread the fruits of Christian folly,
And this stubborn melancholy
Fond of life and liberty.
Chains and dungeons ye are wooing,
And the storm of death pursuing;
Rebels to the known decree.[1]

Theater director Peter Sellars, noted for contemporary staging of classical operas and plays, presented *Theodora*, to great acclaim, at the 1996 Glyndebourne Festival outside London. In this version Antioch was contemporary America. Valens was president, as cocksure and mocking as our current president, Donald J. Trump. Theodora was a penitent socialite who, at her conversion, removed her earrings and necklace. The soldiers were dressed in a manner that mirrored a combination of storm troopers and SWAT teams, an American flag sewn high on their right arms.

The scene, for me, was hyperbole for the American church's allegiance to empire and our nation's current wave of triumphal exceptionalism. Since 2000, a majority of white Christians have supported the presidential candidates who most reflect nationalist fervor; 81 percent of white evangelicals supported Donald Trump in the 2016 election.[2] The message implicit in the polling data, and explicit in the discourse of the majority of American Christians, is for the mainline church to get over its stubborn melancholy. Enough with the bleeding-heart, do-gooder thing.

However, many predominately white churches have not abandoned their melancholy and are in fact solidifying and expanding its significance and reach within their communities. The still point of their life together is lament. I am acquainted with one such

---

[1] Georg Friedrich Händel, *Theodora,* scene 5. The libretto is available at opera.stanford.edu/iu/libretti/theodora.htm.

[2] Jessica Martínez and Gregory A. Smith, "How the Faithful Voted: A Preliminary 2016 Analysis," Pew Research Center (November 9, 2016).

church, Emmanuel Church in Boston. I first present my history with Emmanuel and then describe four dynamic elements of lament that I mine from Emmanuel's history and character: (1) carrying on, (2) just talking with people, (3) moving over and around;, and (4) staying put. The four elements constitute a *collect*, a prayer that gathers and offers to God a compilation of what we have experienced on our journey through the book. They compose a painting, a canvas of lament for Christian community.

## Emmanuel Church and Me: Two Dilemmas in Search of Each Other

In the words of Peter Sellars:

> I was adopted when I was 21 by a group of musicians in Boston at Emmanuel Church. At Emmanuel, they sang the complete Bach cantatas. A cantata in the Sunday service for 35 years. . . . It wasn't until 10 years at Emmanuel that I got this music as not abstract at all. . . . It really engages people's lives. At the time, Emmanuel had a homeless shelter, AA groups, a Salvadorian refugee program. The reason Bach makes the most extreme demands of the instrumentalists and the vocalists is because changing your life is really hard. You think you can move forward but then you go back and you think you're making progress but then you lose the way again. Then these amazing moments of harmonic convergence where even when you stumble, actually the harmony tells you you're coming home. And that you shouldn't give up, you should keep going. I feel something drawing me on and that's Bach's harmonic universe. These incredible convergences were really deep when we were performing this material in the context of broken lives. And when you hear Bach Cantata 199 after

convincing someone not to kill themselves, you get that this music is deeply practical.[3]

Emmanuel Church was my halfway house.

I came to Emmanuel as priest-in-charge in 1993 and was elected rector in 1995. A few months before my arrival at Emmanuel, I wrote to my bishop and shared that I was ready to consider a return to parish ministry. I had spent eight years in hospice communities serving the underserved and maligned in Atlanta and Boston. I was exhausted, not because of the people we served, but by the healthcare environment through which we served them. As leader of the hospices, my primary responsibility was to protect the people we served from a healthcare environment and culture that in many ways erased them.

My bishop asked me to serve Emmanuel. It was a parish on the rocks. Ostensibly, the issue was the music program. Some of the parishioners thought the music program, particularly the cantatas, had taken over the parish. The matter became irreconcilable under the current congregational leadership and structure. The bishop called the parish back to mission status, under his direct control. The bishop thought that the parish and I would be a good match through the transition process and until the parish returned to full congregational status. Previously I had been a Lutheran pastor, well acquainted with and a lover of the sacred music of Bach, who was a devout Lutheran. And I had experience leading organizations through crisis. My first Sunday at Emmanuel the member appointed to welcome worshipers said, "Welcome to Emmanuel Church in the City of Boston [official name of the parish], the second oldest church in Boston's Back Bay and the newest mission

---

[3] The excerpt is from an interview with Peter Sellars about his staging of the Bach *Saint Matthew Passion* in collaboration with the Berlin Philharmonic Orchestra and the Berlin Radio Choir, available on YouTube.

of the Episcopal Diocese of Massachusetts." A dicey and delicate community.

The people of Emmanuel, the people Emmanuel served, and the Eucharist, with cantata, offered the refreshment I desired and the nourishment I needed to transition from a worn-out health-care administrator to a presider at the altar and pastor of a flock. As mentioned earlier, my eight years among the indigent poor and the Missing Generation, the 235,000 people who died from AIDS in America before it became a more chronic disease, were saturated with radical community. Emmanuel was edgy enough to provide the kind of transitional space I needed to make my way back to mainline Christianity. I needed a community that would understand and even celebrate the fact that, metaphorically, in the narthexes of the churches I had served there were baskets of colored condoms and bottles of bleach for cleaning hypodermic needles. A church less progressive than Emmanuel would have been too much of a culture shock.

The cantata program at Emmanuel remains, soon to celebrate fifty years of service to the wider Boston community. During my twelve years at Emmanuel the cantatas served as an icon through which I prayed the brokenness of myself, the parish, and the world. The cantatas are psalmic language, the trajectory of wailing-lament-solidarity-joy-justice, the movement which, as I have noted throughout the book, is at the heart of salvation history. Moreover, during my tenure Peter Sellars staged two cantatas with Emmanuel, Cantata 82, *I Have Enough*, and Cantata 199, *My Heart Swims in Blood*. I continue to pray these stubbornly melancholic testimonial performances as a protest of the American church's theology of glory and the boisterous and bold xenophobia of a significant portion of the American populace.

Emmanuel's servant ministry continues to grow in numerous directions that make a great difference for the good. In the

mid-1990s, Emmanuel sponsored the Rev. Debbie Little for ordination. Just before and during Debbie's ordination process, she
founded *common cathedral* (Ecclesia Ministries, Inc.), "an outdoor
church for people experiencing homelessness, and their friends."
Its website further states:

> *common cathedral* (Ecclesia Ministries, Inc.) is an outdoor con-
> gregation, housed and un-housed, sharing God's love through
> community, pastoral care, creative expression, and worship on
> Boston Common. We are non-proselytizing and ecumenical.
> We welcome and support all people.

Ecclesia Ministries, Inc., which is housed at Emmanuel Church, has
collaborated with many cities across the United States to start ministries grounded in the same mission as *common cathedral*. Two other
Ecclesia Ministries programs are offered at Emmanuel: *common art*, a
Wednesday afternoon community of unhoused and housed people
making art together; and Boston Warm, an emergency-relief day
center for people without shelter.

In 1997, Emmanuel Church collaborated with the City of
Boston, the Massachusetts Department of Mental Health, and a
not-for-profit mental health agency to establish the Safe Haven
Shelter for Women in a portion of the expansive basement of
the church.

> The Safe Haven Shelter for Women is a transitional shelter
> open 24 hours/day for homeless women with severe and per-
> sistent mental illness living on the streets in Back Bay, Boston
> Common, and Downtown Crossing. The shelter provides
> daytime drop-in services and overnight accommodations
> for six adult women. The program also offers nursing assess-
> ment, counseling, case management, housing and entitlement

linkage, meals, and laundry. Our goal is to assist residents in finding permanent supportive housing.[4]

In 2004, Emmanuel Church made a home for and continues to share a ministry with a Reform Jewish community, Boston Jewish Spirit, now organized as Central Reform Temple. Presently, the Onnuri i:um Chapel Korean Presbyterian Campus Ministry and Universal Worship in Boston: A Celebration of One Human Family reside at Emmanuel.

Other programs continue to prosper. For decades the Back Alley Puppet Theater and Free Puppet Lending Library have lived in the basement of Emmanuel. A visit there is a journey through the likes of Narnia. And, most days, visitors will find or be surprised by the sudden appearance of Sara Peattie, founder, a sorcerer-like spirit who rivals Yoda in terms of demeanor and presence. Sara creates liturgical art for Emmanuel worship. Her puppets gladden community celebrations throughout New England. Each week there are twenty-two 12-Step meetings at Emmanuel. Three nights a week, there are 11:30 p.m. meetings. There is a weekly senior luncheon for the LGBT community. Entertainment follows each meal, including recitals from the New England Conservatory and Boston Conservatory and a wide variety of guest speakers. The Institute for Justice and Democracy in Haiti is also housed at Emmanuel.

## Emmanuel's History

The present-day vigor of Emmanuel's servant ministry issues from a long history of stubborn melancholy. Four characteristics of Emmanuel's history stand out.

---

[4] Eliot Community Human Services website, "Homeless Services—Safe Haven," www.eliotchs.org.

## Emmanuel Is Progressive

On May 24, 1854, Anthony Burns, a young African American man who worked at a Boston clothing store, was captured on his way home from work. Burns had escaped from slavery in Virginia. His owner tracked him down and had him arrested. Under the Fugitive Slave Act of 1850, Burns had no legal right to resist. Folks in Boston were livid. Some seven thousand Bostonians failed to spring him from jail, and the city's finest lawyers could not make a case for his freedom.[5]

In response to Burns's return to Virginia, Amos Adams Lawrence, from one of Boston's wealthiest and most venerated families, in a letter to his uncle, wrote, "We went to bed one night old-fashioned, conservative, Compromise Union Whigs and waked up stark mad Abolitionists."[6] Amos Adams Lawrence made good on his madness. He spent a great deal of money funding the successful anti-slavery struggle to make the new territory of Kansas a free state; hence, Lawrence, Kansas, home of the University of Kansas. Lawrence's largesse was funded from the bounty of the family's textile business, mostly sourced from cotton, "which was planted, picked, ginned, baled, and shipped by slaves."[7] The irony did not seem to disturb Lawrence.

Emmanuel Church in the City of Boston was formed March 17, 1860, in the home of Dr. William Lawrence, 98 Beacon Street. William was the brother of Amos Adams. Emmanuel began as a community of mostly elite abolitionists. Later in the nineteenth century, Harriet Beecher Stowe's daughters were confirmed at Emmanuel.

---

[5] Robert K. Sutton, "The Bostonian Who Armed the Anti-Slavery Settlers in 'Bleeding Kansas,'" Zócalo Public Square: Ideas Journalism with a Head and Heart, August 8, 2017.

[6] Ibid.

[7] Ibid.

Beginning in the 1960s, Emmanuel became more decidedly progressive through the ministry of its ninth rector, the Rev. Al Kershaw. The Rev. Kershaw, before arriving at Emmanuel, was a winner on the television show *The $64,000 Question*. He donated the prize money to civil rights organizations, most of it to the NAACP. The Rev. Kershaw drew the ire of white supremacists around the nation. In 1956, the governor of Mississippi intervened to force the chaplain of the University of Mississippi to rescind the invitation to the Rev. Kershaw to deliver the keynote address during Religious Emphasis Week. When the Rev. Kershaw arrived at Emmanuel, and during his first few years of ministry, a good number of more wealthy members, and their pledges, migrated to other Episcopal parishes in and outside the city. Emmanuel remains one of the most progressive parishes in the Episcopal Diocese of Massachusetts.

## Emmanuel Prays the Contradictions of Lived Experience

Amos Adams Lawrence and his kin made money off the institution of slavery and used the money against the institution of slavery. The deep contradictions of life are rarely resolved. Research on our own lived experience reveals the incongruities of our values and actions. I detest war—and I pay taxes to support approximately eight hundred US military bases in over seventy countries.[8] I found Emmanuel to be particularly adept at embracing the paradoxes of lived experience. We named the enigmas of faith with a curiosity that evoked contemplation and action. That I pay my taxes and make monthly contributions to the Southern Poverty Law Center reflects Emmanuel's prayerfulness.

---

[8] David Vine, "Where in the World Is the US Military?," *Politico Magazine* (July/August 2014).

## Emmanuel Is Open

Emmanuel's first rector was the Rev. Frederic Dan Huntington. He arrived as a Unitarian and shortly thereafter was ordained into the Episcopal Church. Emmanuel's religious border remains porous. During the "time of troubles," the manner in which parishioners remember the controversy that precipitated my ministry at Emmanuel, the parish was called out by a priest of the diocese for having a "Jew on the vestry." Craig Smith, the music director and founder of the cantata program, was cited by others in the diocese for "not believing Jesus to be the Son of God." During the Rev. Kershaw's ministry the parish did away with the membership role. Decades ago the parish's slogan, before such language became trendy, was "Welcome wherever you are on your spiritual journey." Many among the flock added, "wherever you are, or are not, on your spiritual journey." Porous religious borders within the parish environment create safer space for a variety of people and perspectives, commitments, and values that vivify parish life and make for heartier lamentational relation. I find that religious belief often is too high a mountain from which to lament. The air oftentimes is too thin for lament's interchanges and offerings of vulnerability, doubt, and uncertainty. Lament breathes better in the lowlands.

## Emmanuel Is Pioneering

It follows that a historically progressive, open Christian community that invites dialogue about the ambiguities and contradictions of lived experience would be innovative. It is not a coincidence that Emmanuel hosts twenty-two 12-Step meetings a week. Such stubborn melancholy stems from a particularly robust chapter in Emmanuel's history, what the contemporary press named the Emmanuel movement.

The movement began in 1906, during the tenure of Emmanuel's fourth rector, the Rev. Dr. Elwood Worcester. The Rev. Worcester and the assistant rector, the Rev. Samuel McComb, hosted group meetings at the church for persons suffering from diseases occasioned by "poverty, malnutrition and crowding," such as "tuberculosis . . . present in virtually epidemic proportions, and syphilis or typhus, called 'social diseases' because of the conditions under which they flourished." The meetings were "offered to the public, free of charge, open to all social classes and individuals of any religious denomination or of no religion at all."[9] The Emmanuel movement flourished for roughly six years, until the medical community's ongoing rants about "who can do what" took a toll. Nonetheless, the ministry continued in one form or another until 1929, when the Rev. Worcester completed his ministry at Emmanuel. The Emmanuel movement is noted for being a precursor of group therapy and Alcoholics Anonymous. More about the Emmanuel movement later.

Emmanuel celebrated its first same-sex commitment ceremony in 1981. In 2004, with the parish's strong support, including a letter to the standing committee of the diocese, I defied my bishop by solemnizing three same-sex marriages of parishioners shortly after same-sex marriage was legalized in Massachusetts. My defiance was not a renegade act. The parish and I loved our bishop. We sweated through a defiance of our bishop's decision to obey his bishops, the presiding bishop of the American church and the Archbishop of Canterbury. The final paragraph of the vestry's letter stated:

"Must grace fall so unevenly on the earth?" the playwright Tony Kushner has asked. We fellow children of Eve have no easy answer to that hard question. But we know that we

---

[9] Sanford Gifford, *The Emmanuel Movement: The Origins of Group Treatment and the Assault on Lay Psychotherapy* (Boston: The Harvard University Press for the Francis Countway Library of Medicine, 1997), 23, 1.

have been given our voices to affirm that all are called, all are chosen. And we rest our uncertain hearts in Kushner's small prayer, "I almost know you are there. I think you are our home."

Emmanuel's history created and continues to sustain an environment inviting of and fruitful for lamentational relation. My participation in her stubborn melancholy, following years at Grady Hospital and the Hospice at Mission Hill, helped shape what I have determined to be the four foundational elements of lament that enliven Christian community.

## Carrying On

Linda was part of the first cohort of unhoused women who lived at Safe Haven. Linda's first engagement with the Emmanuel community was at the Thursday evening Eucharist, which was held in the chapel, a smaller venue. The chapel is dedicated to the women martyrs of the church. Statues of the women martyrs make up the ornamental backdrop behind the altar. I like to think that the womanly atmosphere of the chapel made it a safer place for Linda to venture into relation with parishioners.

Linda sat in the back of the chapel, several rows from other parishioners. During the sharing of the peace, a parishioner came toward her, extended his hand, and said, "The peace of the Lord be with you." Linda screamed, "Don't touch me!" and fled worship. In a few weeks Linda returned. She sat alone, and parishioners let her be. A few weeks later Linda came forward for communion wearing a red mitt on her right hand. She received the bread.

As time passed Linda mingled more and more with parishioners. After a few years, during an adult-education event following worship, Linda interrupted the conversation, saying, "Linda is not my real name. My name is Sharon." Over the years, until Sharon's death,

Emmanuel and Sharon slowly choreographed a way to be together that enabled the distinction of Sharon-Emmanuel to fade to the background. Sharon emerged as a participant in the community, to whom the Emmanuel community paid particular, more focused attention in order for her to be as safe as possible.

When Sharon was dismissed from Safe Haven for breaking rules, people from Emmanuel worked to acquire for her a single occupancy room in the city. They arranged rides to and from worship. Sharon eventually shared that she had a sister. The rector of the parish, the Rev. Pamela Werntz, encouraged Sharon to contact her sister. Her sister had presumed that Sharon was dead. When Sharon was no longer able to live alone, her sister found her a new home, an assisted-living center where she lived until she died.

A particular experience serves as an icon expressive of Sharon's place in the Emmanuel community and Emmanuel's place in Sharon's life. An extended quote from Pam's homily at Sharon's burial service states:

> When things weren't going Sharon's way (and they rarely were), she was likely to create quite a scene. Heaven help the unsuspecting kind stranger who would try to gently guide Sharon or offer physical assistance when she was moving at a glacial pace or seemed unsteady on her feet. I don't think anyone ever tried to touch her arm more than once. Except. Except, there was the time that Wendy Grew, wife of retired Bishop Clark Grew, got a cup of lemonade after church one Sunday and took it over to Sharon and offered it to her. Sharon started screaming, "What makes you think that I would accept that from you? I have no idea who has touched that. It could be contaminated." And so forth. Everyone in the back of chapel took a few steps back, shocked at the noise that Sharon was making, everyone, that is, except Wendy. Wendy calmly waited for Sharon to stop yelling and said sweetly,

"Well, I will tell you why I brought you lemonade. It's because that's what friends do." Sharon was very surprised. She
muttered, "You're my friend?" And Wendy said "I thought we
were friends because last week I helped you across the street
when you were afraid, and helped you get on the T to go
home." Sharon raised her head and asked, "That was you?"
And then she took the lemonade and said thank you.

Lament does not depend on or expect that extending a guarded
hand toward the Body of Christ means that persons may become
less guarded and more comfortable with one another, though that is
often a gift of lament. A mitted hand is emblematic and expressive
of persons reaching for riskier relation and co-creating ways to participate and remain in it. Community is strengthened, and persons
who constitute community may or may not be changed. Stronger
community does not signify that people are made better as a result
of it. Persons are blessed by community. Blessing and *metanoia* are
cousins but not twins. The promise of community without the
expectation of transformation is the grace of carrying on.

## Just Talking with People

Often during family therapy sessions at the Salem Center, where
I trained and worked, it was hard to distinguish between family
members and the therapist. Family therapists Harlene Anderson
and Harry Goolishian, cited in previous chapters, write: "We de-
nounced ourselves as therapists. We described what we did as *just
talking with people*."[10]

"Just talking with people" is not dumbing down therapy, as the
modernist institution of therapy initially argued in its objectification

---

[10] Harlene Anderson, *Conversation, Language, and Possibility: A Postmodern Approach to Therapy* (New York: Basic Books, 1997), 67.

of the postmodern therapy movement. Just talking with people, as mentioned in previous chapters, flattens the hierarchy of expertise and redistributes it among all who participate in the conversation. All are learners and co-creators of new knowledge for life-in-relation. If such a therapy session seems similar to a walk with a friend around Jamaica Pond in Boston, that's because it is.

The mental-health industrial complex's size is not indicative of its merit. Its size, in part, is related to our culture's professionalization of love. Sigmund Freud had this to say about the Emmanuel movement's layperson-led success at equipping and empowering those at and over the margins of daily life to carry on:

> The Emmanuel movement, which, however, I have not had time to study carefully, will die down as have so many other movements. When I think that there are many physicians who have been studying modern methods of psychotherapy for decades, and who yet practice it only with the greatest caution, this introduction of a few men without medical or with only superficial medical training seems to me at the very least of questionable good. I can easily understand that the combination of church and psychotherapy appeals to the public, for the public has always had a certain weakness for everything that savors of mysteries and the mysterious, and these it probably suspects behind psychotherapy, which in reality has nothing, absolutely nothing mysterious about it.[11]

The nature of Freud's assessment persists.

Moreover, our society's preoccupation with self-actualization and self-sufficiency leaves little time or energy for what once was more likely to transpire on front porches and in church meeting rooms. We have farmed out care. I greatly respect hospice and honor the

---

[11] In Gifford, *The Emmanuel Movement*, 85–86.

great difference it makes in the lives of dying people and their loved ones. Nonetheless, hospice volunteers do what family members and parishioners once did. Congregations reside closer to the margins of care of the dying. Congregations mostly provide the liturgical interlude at the time of death, along with a lot of food and more than usual visitation for roughly ten days after the death.

Christian communities struggle to realize the remarkable difference for the good lamentational relation and conversation make in the lives of parishioners. The ascendancy of professional love and farmed-out care makes it harder for us to imagine that we really are balm for broken hearts, soothers of anxiety, bearers of hope, and prophets in a society too autonomous for its own good. Our culturally infused inferiority moves us to put our relational lights under a bushel more often than on a stand (Mt 5:15).

Many years ago, after seminary, I entered a clergy climate in which there was a hierarchical distinction between clergy who did and did not have specialized training. Clergy without additional training offered from secular institutions felt objectified by modernist manners that, as Freud wrote, passed us off as those dealing in passe mysteries. We could *just talk* with people, unlike certified and licensed listeners. We sometimes felt that parishioners sought us out because they were intimidated by, scared of, or not able to afford psychotherapy. I also believe that often we were too quick to reach for the Rolodex when we were approached to care for and cure souls.

I sense that the modernist shaming of the Christian mysteries is waning a bit. I believe that the reign of the therapeutic is in slow decline. Life after Freud isn't what it used to be. I also sense that Christian and other religious communities, and those who facilitate life within them, are gaining confidence in the power and significance of the conversational partnerships they create and sustain. We are beginning to discover what the psychotherapy world knows but is slow to confess; namely, the "therapeutic alliance," a heady phrase for the relational bond between conversational partners, accounts for most of the good that comes from talk therapy. William James, an ardent supporter of the Emmanuel movement, was prescient in regard to the therapeutic alliance, observing, "The therapeutic relation may be what we can only at present describe as a relation of one person to another."[12]

Relational bonding is more art than science, more gift than skill. Slowly, ever so slowly, the therapeutic temples of love and care are starting to laicize. The *cura animarum* (cure of souls) is returning home. *Ecclesia* and clinic are becoming more like than unlike. And, unlike the Emmanuel movement's struggles with the medical establishment and press, professional healers and the general public are starting to be more curious, less cautious about the role religious communities play in the wellness movement. The more lamentational relations and conversations Christian communities offer, the greater confidence and ability we have to claim our authority.

## Moving Over and Around

Several weeks ago I interviewed Pamela Werntz, still the rector of Emmanuel, and her wife, Joy Howard, to catch up on life at Emmanuel. A lot is happening. I asked Pam how she managed so many groups of people *just talking* with one another during most hours of the day and night. Pam said that she does not manage them and would not manage them if she could.

Pam shared the parish's key policy: "Respecting the intent of anonymity, Emmanuel does not require surnames to be given in order to acquire keys to the building, only reliable contact information." Most of the churches I served prior to and after Emmanuel

---

[12] William James correspondence: G. Stanley Hall to James, 27 December 1879 and James to Hall, 16 January 1880. Quoted in Ralph Barton Perry, *The Thought and Character of William James*, 2 vols. (Boston: Little, Brown, and Co., 1935), 2:1–19, cited in Gifford, *The Emmanuel Movement*, 24–25.

would consider such a key policy irresponsible. We obsess about keys—who has them and how to get them back when someone leaves the vestry or church. After all, "we could never replace the chalices if they were stolen. They would cost a fortune, and the Stewart family gave them to the church!"

I imagine Pam and the vestry of Emmanuel understand their policy to be responsible, less faithful to good order but more faithful to *ecclesia*. They trust that groups have the wherewithal to manage themselves and their relations with other groups. Such trust makes for more open borders. Borders between worship, meeting, and administrative spaces bend and flow. The border between the inside and outside of the building is porous. In the spirit of Derrida's vision of impossible hospitality, examined in Chapter 6, persons moving around in the building and moving in and out of the building are not beholden to Emmanuel as guests are to hosts. The dynamic of host and guest softens. The distinction between who does and does not belong and the hierarchy of belonging—priest-vestry-member-guest-visitor—fades. The building is a roof over, a door to, community. Building as sacrament.

William Cavanaugh, reflecting on the Roman Catholic Church in Chile during the early years of the Pinochet dictatorship, writes:

> The Eucharist produces a radical identification of three terms: Christ, those who suffer, and me (cf. Matthew 25:31–46). This we need to proclaim boldly, if the church is to heal the fragmentation of the world. To proclaim it, though, is more than a verbal act. It requires making the body of Christ visible through concrete practices. In Chile this began with the simple act of making the church a place where people could gather. At a time when secular organizations of any kind fell under suspicion and ban, the church used its moral authority to offer workers' cooperatives, soup kitchens, women's groups, legal assistance for victims of oppression, job training, groups

for relatives of political prisoners, and much more. Despite the harassment this invited, the church understood that being an alternative social body was the realization of the Eucharist imperative to be what we receive, to become the body of Christ and allow others to feed on us.[13]

## Staying Put

. . . despite the harassment this invited.

One of the worst church-related meetings I facilitated over the course of my almost four decades of ministry was the Back Bay community meeting to discuss the establishment of Safe Haven in Emmanuel's basement. The hardest parts of the meeting were the pleas, threats, and diatribes thrown from mostly progressive home-owners in the first block of Commonwealth Avenue, the alley of which abuts Emmanuel. The managers/owners of the high-end boutiques and salons in the first block of Newbury Street, Em-manuel's address, were a bit nicer than the Commonwealth Avenue folks, but NIMBY ("not in my backyard") was still the voiced message.

Many of the boutique and salon folks eventually came around. Some did so in a big way—clothes for residents from the boutiques and personal-care products from the salons. But some of the Com-monwealth Avenue residents continued to complain throughout the rest of my ministry at Emmanuel. According to Pam, a bit of carping from across the alley continues to this day.

How did I stay put in the meeting? How did the congregation remain faithful to the project after the meeting? We had a lot of support. The spirit of those who had died on our watch surrounded us. Ronald and Gladys stood by my side. Ronald was a middle-aged

---

[13] William Cavanaugh, "The Body of Christ: The Eucharist and Politics," *Word and World* 22, no. 2 (Spring 2002): 176.

man from "the projects" in Atlanta, a Grady patient. Gladys was his wife. I hung out with Ronald while he worked on his car. I sat in the kitchen while Gladys cooked supper. And Richard watched my back. A baritone in the Emmanuel choir, he died at Mission Hill before I knew anything about Emmanuel. Christopher Roos, the parish administrator at Emmanuel during my first years there, who died from AIDS before Safe Haven was in the works, infiltrated vestry meetings to encourage us when fear and doubt mired the discourse.

Lamentational relation creates tension and conflict among neighbors inside and with neighbors outside the walls of Christian community. Isaiah's peaceable reign (Is 11:6–9) stirs up trouble. Such is life, especially life right now in "these dread latter days of the old violent beloved U.S.A., in the Christ-forgetting Christ-haunted death–dealing Western World."[14] Memories of our salvation history that are dangerous to empire empower us to stand firm. Lamentational conversations that lessen empire's hold on us inspire us to persist. Iterations of stubborn melancholy shorten the half-life of empire. The more we carry on, the more we *just talk* with one another, the more we move over and around to make room for one another, the more we stay put, the more we will inch empire toward the good. And our relational provocations are prismed, refracted to delight as much as disturb. Artisans of lament are shrewdly strategic, "wise as serpents, innocent as doves" (Mt 10:16). I trust our tears slowly sing empire to sleep.

## Eucharist and Lament

The fourfold art of lament described above is a fledgling contribution to a nascent ecclesiology for Christian community that

---

[14] Walker Percy, *Love in the Ruins* (New York: Farrar, Straus and Giroux, 1971), 3.

labors under the ambient light of the American empire. We need to see the stars again. Vincent Van Gogh's *Starry Night* is our proper sanctuary. The prayerful question: How do we move Christian community, figuratively speaking, from empire's glare to Maine's Piscataquis County—our smallest county, population 17,000, only two stop lights, five hundred feet apart. There the night sky astounds and delights.

Our ecclesiology begins small and remains simple. No need to invent and imagine new ways to endure the weight of enlivening and inspiring communities to carry on. *Just talk* with one another, move over and around for one another, stay put with one another. The art of lament is less a weighty means of grace and more a sublime infection spread at a common table of un-sanitized hands and hearts—Eucharist. Eucharist is our starry night. Piscataquis County is our altar.

By small and simple I mean a radical reorientation of our lived theology of Eucharist. As William T. Cavanaugh suggests,[15] we let go of the notion that Eucharist is what the church performs as a spiritual elixir for her constituents. We embrace Eucharist as that which performs church through the drama of wailing-lament-solidarity-joy-justice. We deconstruct Eucharist from being a collection of empire-weary souls receiving a rationed balm, performing a duty required, swallowing a prescription to ease angst, hoping to become different from what we are. We reconstruct Eucharist, as it has always been, broken and bent bodies, just as we are, in relation time after time, again and again.

Around the common table, tears sing. Lament is the open and outstretched arms of Eucharist.

---

[15] William T. Cavanaugh, *Torture and Eucharist* (Malden, MA: Blackwell Publishing, 1998), 235.

Epilogue

# The Community of Saints

*Behold who you are. May we become what we receive.*[1]

At the end of a Sunday night Eucharist at Emmanuel the usher handed me a few wadded-up dollar bills offered during the collection. The usher said that he did not know if he should have taken the money. The money was a gift from an unhoused man who spent many days and nights on the steps of the church.

The next morning I handed the wad of bills to Christopher, our parish administrator. Christopher was a good friend. Christopher was a wonderful mess, iconoclastic and godly to the core. Christopher had a way of teaching me a lot about God at moments that mattered. I told Christopher that I felt I was holding something holy. I wasn't sure what to do with it. Christopher responded by inviting me to go with him to the Busch Reisinger Museum at Harvard University. We went the next afternoon.

Christopher led me to a sculpture by Ernst Barlach titled *The Crippled Beggar*. The story behind the sculpture is as compelling as the work itself. Completed in 1930, the sculpture is of a haggard

---

[1] Words spoken by the celebrant during Eucharist, before the distribution of the elements, at Emery House, the rural retreat of the Society of Saint John the Evangelist, a monastic community of the Anglican tradition, in Cambridge, Massachusetts.

man on crutches with upturned face and eyes. According to the museum gallery's text, the work "was commissioned for a niche high on the fourteenth-century brick facade of the former Church of St. Catherine in Lübeck, Germany. Although sixteen figures were originally planned, protests from reactionary critics and lack of funding stymied the project, and Barlach completed only three." The title of the commission was *The Community of Saints.* The National Socialists called Barlach's work a mockery of the Divine. I like to imagine a sixteen-member lament choir carrying on to-gether, *just talking*, making room and staying put for one another, slowly singing empire to sleep.

The works of Barlach were included in the *Entartete Kunst*, the degenerate art exhibition, which opened in Munich on July 19, 1937. Important works were collected from public museums for the presentation. The art was assembled for the purpose of clarifying for the German people what type of modern art was unacceptable. Barlach died in 1938, a year after he was informed that he would no longer be allowed to exhibit. Barlach was said to be un-German, Slavic, unbalanced, and a lunatic.

Christopher was being Christopher. The visit to the museum reminded me that the man who handed us a wad of bills disturbs my sometimes more glorified image of the community of saints.

Back to the photograph, mentioned in Chapter 5, of the young girl posing beside a loom in a western North Carolina cotton mill. The photo rests in the window sill just to the right of my computer screen. The young girl has stood watch throughout this writing project. Her presence helped prism the grind of writing into lamentational prayer. She testifies. I witness. She is an icon through whom I honor my mill village ancestors. Granted, not many starving children with swollen bellies will be fed through my genuflections. Still, our testifier-witness relation sanctifies. Her testimony brings the community of saints down to earth and into the moment.

Association with disenfranchised people is less a matter of ethics and more a function of location. Presence with put-down and put-upon people is not so much a concern about what the church does but rather an indicator of where the church is. The church's fidelity with the broken and bent ones is not a medium for our largesse but a mark of our existence. Church is the broken and bent ones. Church is the crippled beggar.

Jürgen Moltmann writes: *ubi Christus, ibi ecclesia.*[2] Where Christ is, there is the church. Not where the church is, there is Christ. Where Christ is, there is the church. That Christ has always been with the least as the least is, for me, the most predictable characteristic of Christ and the best clue I have in regard to the whereabouts of the church. Christ and the church are as bound to the marginalized and erased as the Red Sox are to Fenway Park.

Such a criterion at first glance suggests an exclusionary smear on the God business, as if only outcasts are in the club. Before we shout, "What am I, chopped liver!?" remember that chopped liver is probably something we are more like than not. Who among us has not spent time in the desert of disconsolation? Who among us has not spent a good amount of time in the valley of the shadow of death? When I am particularly blue and afraid, I ride around in my newer Toyota Tacoma listening to Bach and Johnny Cash. The living God visits us at those places where we are lame. The church is where tears sing.

Our lives are a widow's mite. We have so little to give. We have so much solidarity to gain. Church is about relation, lamentational relation, among God and neighbor. God and neighbor, neighbor and God. Pray it both ways, as a litany, over and over. The distinction between them dissolves.

---

[2] Jürgen Moltmann, *The Church in the Power of the Spirit: A Contribution to Messianic Ecclesiology* (Minneapolis: Fortress Press, 1993), 123.

# Permissions

*(continued from the copyright page)*

Reprinted by permission of Farrar, Straus and Giroux:

- Excerpt from SMILLA'S SENSE OF SNOW by Peter Høeg, translated by Tiina Nunnally. Translation copyright © 1993 by Farrar, Straus and Giroux, LLC. Reprinted by permission of Farrar, Straus and Giroux.
- Excerpt from "The Legend of Tucker Caliban" from SEEDS OF DESTRUCTION by Thomas Merton. Copyright © 1964 by The Abbey of Gethsemani. Copyright renewal 1992 by Robert Giroux, James Laughlin, and Tommy O'Callaghan.
- Excerpts from "Revelation" from THE COMPLETE STORIES by Flannery O'Connor. Copyright © 1971 by the Estate of Mary Flannery O'Connor.
- Excerpt from MYSTERY AND MANNERS by Flannery O'Connor, edited by Sally and Robert Fitzgerald. Copyright © 1969 by the Estate of Mary Flannery O'Connor.

Excerpts from OPEN CLOSED OPEN: Poems by Yehuda Amichai, translated from the Hebrew by Chana Bloch and Chana Kronfeld. Copyright © 2000 by Chana Bloch and Chana Kronfeld. Used by permission of Houghton Mifflin Harcourt Publishing Company. All rights reserved.

Excerpts from *The Fire Next Time* by James Baldwin. Copyright © 1962, 1963 by James Baldwin. Copyright renewed. Published by Vintage Books. Used by arrangement with the James Baldwin Estate.

Excerpts from LETTERS AND PAPERS FROM PRISON, REVISED, ENLARGED ED. by Dietrich Bonhoeffer, translated from the German by R. H. Fuller, Frank Clark, et al. Copyright © 1953, 1967, 1971 by SCM Press Ltd. Reprinted with the permission of Scribner, a division of Simon & Schuster, Inc. All rights reserved.

Excerpts from JOY UNSPEAKABLE: Contemplative Practices of the Black Church, by Barbara A. Holmes. Copyright © 2017 by Fortress Press. Reprinted with the permission of 1517 Media, of which Fortress Press is an imprint.

Excerpts from "Chapter 6: Pray for Your Own Discovery" by Thomas Merton, from NEW SEEDS OF CONTEMPLATION, copyright © 1961 by The Abbey of Gethsemani, Inc. Reprinted by permission of New Directions Publishing Corp.

Excerpt(s) from ABIDE WITH ME: A NOVEL by Elizabeth Strout, copyright © 2006 by Elizabeth Strout. Used by permission of Random House, an imprint and division of Penguin Random House LLC. All rights reserved.

Excerpt from NO FUTURE WITHOUT FORGIVENESS by Desmond Tutu, copyright © 1999 by Desmond Tutu. Used by permission of Doubleday, an imprint of the Knopf Doubleday Publishing Group, a division of Penguin Random House LLC. All rights reserved.

Excerpt from KADDISH by Leon Wieseltier, copyright © 2000 by Leon Wieseltier. Used by permission of Vintage, a company of Penguin Random House LLC. All rights reserved.

Excerpts from *Finding Beauty in a Broken World* by Terry Tempest Williams, copyright © 2008 by Terry Tempest Williams. Used by permission of Brandt & Hochman Literary Agents, Inc. Any copying or distribution of this text is expressly forbidden. All rights reserved.

Portions of William Blaine-Wallace, "The Politics of Tears: Lamentation as Justice-Making," in *Injustice and the Care of Souls: Taking Oppression Seriously in Pastoral Care*, ed. Sheryl A. Kujawa-Holbrook and Karen B. Montagno (Minneapolis: Fortress Press, 2009), have been incorporated into this volume. Used by permission of Fortress Press.

# Index